Drawn Thread Embroidery

Drawn Thread Embroidery

Moyra McNeill

An Owl Book
Henry Holt and Company
New York

Library of Congress Catalog Card Number: 90–81419

ISBN 0–8050–1406–3   (An Owl Book: pbk.)

Henry Holt books are available at special discounts
for bulk purchases for sales promotions, premiums,
fund-raising, or educational use. Special editions
or book excerpts can also be created to specification.

For details contact:

Special Sales Director
Henry Holt and Company, Inc.
115 West 18th Street
New York, New York 10011

First American Edition

Typeset by Latimer Trend & Company Ltd.
Printed in Great Britain
10 9 8 7 6 5 4 3 2 1

Contents

Introduction

'Ah yes', people say when you mention drawn thread, 'I've got some tablecloths my grandmother did, and they are very beautiful, but I never use them nowadays except for very special occasions'. As with many forms of embroidery, drawn thread still projects an image of a past age, irrelevant to modern life. But used in an evolving, modern way, this type of embroidery offers a wide range of lively possibilities, some of which this book will show. In the coming years of shorter working days and lives, the role of embroidery as a satisfying, creative pursuit can certainly be relevant to current needs.

People are deterred from working embroidery, and drawn thread in particular, for a number of reasons. These can be dealt with one by one.

It looks complicated
Many kinds of embroidery look complicated, but when the stages of production are analysed, most techniques are considerably simpler to work than first sight would suggest.

It looks time-consuming
Embroidery is essentially a slow craft, but nowadays embroiderers have a choice between work that grows quickly and work that is meticulous and time-consuming. By using bold fabrics such as furnishing fabrics and hessian, very effective work can be achieved; also, some machine techniques, worked on the domestic sewing machine, can be based on the concepts of withdrawn thread yet developed in quite a different way to the hand techniques.

It has to be in monochrome
Even monochrome need not be boring if the texture is varied; try contrasting shiny, matt, ridged and knobbly, for example. Variation may also be made between holes or spaces of varied or graded sizes, contrasting with areas of plain fabric.

The fabric can also be coloured; in dress and furnishing fabric departments, materials are displayed in ranges of colour, fibre and scale that are quite suitable for drawn thread. White fabrics may be space-dyed, sprayed or sponged with colour to give interesting

1 (opposite) Grandma's teacloth shows well-designed borders with contrasting white surface embroidery in the middle

lively effects; threads also may be coloured or space-dyed to make the work less mechanical and therefore less boring to do (and certainly less boring for the onlooker).

It is too mechanical

In an embroidery method based on holes, such as drawn thread, the emphasis is on the holes rather than the threads of the fabric; these may be greatly varied in size, and need not be regular; they can be created randomly to make the work livelier.

It is irrelevant to modern needs

Again, people tend to refer to past examples and imagine that drawn thread has a limited range of applications, whereas it can be applied to a considerable range of items in a modern context, from very practical pieces to entirely decorative ones, as this book shows.

It is expensive

This illusion is also based on the premise that drawn thread must be worked on fine Irish linen; it does look very handsome in its traditional form, but nowadays may be translated to more readily available fabrics that are more colourful and bolder in scale. Although natural fibres are enjoyable to work with, many synthetic fabrics are more appropriate if the work is to be laundered. Linen was used in the past simply because it was the indigenous fibre, that is, the most readily available.

Traditional threads are no longer available

It is sad for those of us who have had the pleasure of working with the superb quality of lustrous twisted linen threads to find them no longer freely available; but there are many exciting new yarns on the market which have equal power to inspire and enthuse the embroiderer. These can be synthetic cotton, pure silk, woollen mixtures and even some modern linen threads. Throughout history, embroidery has evolved from century to century, due in a large part to the introduction of 'new' materials and threads from other parts of the world. As with all forms of creativity, if ideas remain fixed and static, embroidery will become stultified and the quality of craftwork will degenerate.

It is so boring to work

Only if the worker allows it to be, by not thinking how to vary stitch, thread, and (therefore) texture to make it interesting to do and look at. Once again, the mental image of yards of identically worked borders impinges on what modern embroidery actually is; as embroiderers today we have a background of centuries of ideas to inspire us, but there is no value in copying them slavishly, as their times were very different from ours.

1 Fabrics and threads

Embroidery aims to alter a fabric or enhance its surface in selected areas, in order to create design, pattern and texture. Drawn thread embroidery, where threads, warp, weft or both, are withdrawn from the fabric, has a long history. Traditionally, the remaining threads are twisted, tied, grouped or woven into other threads in order to make patterns of holes in the fabric.

Drawn fabric looks fragile and lace-like, and so in the past it was thought that removing threads weakened the material, which seems logical. As, however, there are so many drawn thread articles extant from past centuries, it seems this is not the case. For example, many of us have in our care table linen which is now a hundred years or more old, yet has many threads withdrawn. While it would probably be unwise to wash this linen regularly in a washing machine, it has survived boiling, bleaching and the application of indifferent ironing implements, and so must be considerably sturdier than it looks. The material is invariably linen, sewn with linen or cotton threads, and says a lot for the longevity of these fibres. On the other hand, we do not know how many of today's synthetics will react to ageing: it may be that some of them may also have inbuilt longevity. When our ancestors were embroidering it seems unlikely that they were aiming to create for posterity; they simply made what was fashionable at the time, using those materials which were available. Today we sometimes seem obsessed with how long our work will last. Rather, why not do as past ages did — that is, work embroidery that is of today, using those fabrics and threads that are available, to express our own creativity and to make articles we want to make.

Materials for drawn thread
The main prerequisite for drawn thread is a fabric from which threads may be easily withdrawn. The qualities to look for are:

- a fabric you can *see easily* without having to resort to use of magnifiers. Very fine fabric can be frustrating to work

- a weave that is not interlocked. If in doubt, experiment by pulling one thread. If it remains fixed and does not pucker up the material, the fabric is not suitable

- a weave that is not too dense: for example, it is possible to withdraw threads from velvet effectively but it needs the boldest kind, with a long pile and thick threads. Look on the reverse to see the thread size

- a plain tabby weave (alternatively one under, one over). Other weaves, for example gaberdine, crêpe and satin, can be withdrawn, but there is an element of experiment

- warp and weft threads that are strong enough to pull out readily. If threads are loosely spun, they tend to part under the pressure of being withdrawn. Some very fine threads sometimes snap easily under pressure. It is, however, possible to withdraw threads that break easily by cutting them every three inches or so, along a border for example, which reduces the amount of pressure

Fibres

Linen is the most obvious fabric fibre to choose, but there are equally successful substitutes. From time to time, depending on fashion trends, dress fabric departments stock 'linen-look' fabrics which are all synthetic, or mixtures of synthetic with natural fibres.

Wool does not seem the most likely of natural fibres to use for drawn thread because its hairy fibres tend to cling to each other, but if a simple tabby weave fabric, such as hopsack or challis, is chosen, it is quite easy to withdraw threads. Even flannel and tweed can be an appropriate choice.

Hessian and sacking, both made of jute, are an excellent base for bold, large-scale work. Colours in hessian can fade comparatively rapidly, so take this into account when making a selection.

Woven silk is available in a range of weights today. Noile has a clear tabby weave, while shantung is much finer and stiffer. Some textured silk fabrics have a very fine warp and a slub weft (threads which have a noticeable thick blob in them from time to time). Withdrawing the warp on these fabrics leaves only the thick threads, while withdrawing the weft leaves only the very fine threads, thus giving a choice of working scale. At the beginning of this century drawn thread was a popular form of dress decoration on silk clothing.

Cotton is also available in a variety of weights, including duck, voile, cheesecloth and poplin, all of which have a tabby weave. Cotton or cotton mixed with synthetic fibres can also be found in heavier weights as furnishing fabrics; some, like hardanger fabric, have a double thread in each direction, but are nonetheless perfectly suitable for drawn thread.

'Synthetics' describes a wide range of filaments, but as a group these lack resilience or 'give' when woven. They are, however, particularly appropriate for an article that is to be laundered frequently.

Besides pure natural fibres and pure synthetics there are many mixtures of the two, which improves laundering qualities. Such fabrics are made in traditional weaves – hopsack, flannel, tweed and gabardine.

Throughout this book the figure captions mention the fabric wherever possible so that the span of choice can be appreciated. As evenweave embroidery fabrics are often expensive and not readily available, the emphasis is placed on suitable alternatives.

Threads
These are as diverse as the fabrics. In general a single thread is easier to work than a stranded one, and it should be in scale with the fabric – a fine thread on a fine material and a bold one on a coarser fabric. There are, however, occasions when a particular textural effect is required which may turn all the rules on their heads!

The following is a selection, rather than a comprehensive list, of threads.

For hand embroidery
Pearl cotton (*coton perlé*) sizes 3, 5, 8, 12 (thick to fine)
Soft embroidery cotton (*Retors à broder*)
Coton à broder
Bold thread   ordinary sewing threads; they can be
Button thread   cotton, synthetic or in the case of
Buttonhole thread   buttonhole twist there is a version in
                             pure silk.
Crochet threads (cotton)
Danish flower threads (cotton)
Knitting yarns
Tapestry wools (Rowan, Appleton)
Silk threads

For machine or fine hand embroidery
Machine embroidery cotton 30 or 50
Ordinary sewing threads
Rayon threads (Madeira and Natesh)
Metal threads (Madeira Astro)
DMC *Fil d'or*
Lace threads

In addition to these, experiment with ribbons, ribbon-like knitting yarns, flat braids and torn strips of fabric. Threads can also be space-dyed, which gives a rainbow effect that can be especially striking in drawn thread work.

2 Basic techniques

Drawn thread is traditionally a counted thread technique; that is, stitches are worked over counted fabric threads in order to be even. On fine fabrics, blocks of threads may be assessed by eye after some practice, which saves time. On bolder fabrics, once a rhythm has been created there is no need to count every single thread, as even blocks of threads can usually be gauged accurately by eye.

I feel it is best initially to be instructed in a formal procedure, to learn the basis of a technique and to gain confidence. After this, as much licence as possible, by way of free stitching and experiment, can be taken to interpret contemporary design concepts.

Texture is a word used to describe surfaces which can be felt, whether rough, smooth, knobbly, ridged and so on. Embroidering involves building texture, and if we control and think about the textures we are creating, the finished piece is likely to be more effective. Drawn thread involves both texture and pattern; the twisting, tying and knotting of threads in groups creates a raised texture, whereas the holes that are created make a very positive geometric pattern.

Embroidery is always more interesting both to do and to look at if the work is not too mechanical; for example, a ladder hem repeats only one shape and texture, and if used alone could look boring. Examples from the past are attractive because they combine as many as three borders in different widths and use different pattern constructions within each border. Sometimes the borders are contrasted with plain white surface embroidery of floral motifs worked in satin stitch, stem stitch and buttonhole in the centre of the cloth. Quite unconsciously, these embroiderers were adept at controlling texture, thereby creating interesting and lively designs. While the purpose of modern embroidery is changed, it is still possible to learn much from past work in this respect.

Beginning drawn thread borders
The first stage is to withdraw threads from the material. Decide on the area from which they are to be removed and mark the shape outline with either tacking or a water-soluble marker. When a specific number of threads is required, tack a set number, for

example four, under and over to make counting easier.

If a border is to go around four sides of a rectangle or square, begin in the centre of each side to ensure the corners match. Find this by counting threads or by folding the fabric in half; mark it clearly. When counting a very long border, put a pin in after every ten or twenty threads for easier counting.

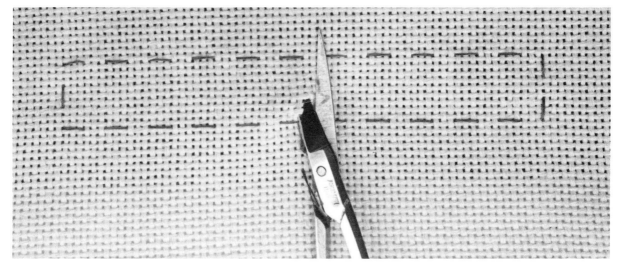

Using a sharp pair of pointed scissors, cut through the threads in the centre of the border. Withdraw the threads to the end (or corner); a tapestry needle is useful for prising them out. Pinch the material at the end of the border between thumb and forefinger of the left hand to make sure the threads do not pull out further than required. These ends now have to be secured. There are a number of ways of doing this:

2 A border outlined with tacking over and under three threads; the scissors are starting to cut the threads in the middle

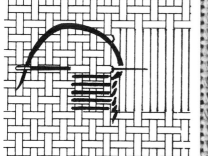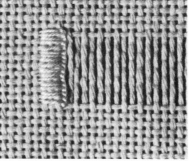

3a Buttonhole being worked to secure the end

3b Finished buttonholing

(a) Buttonhole stitch. Use a pointed needle and a thread slightly finer than one thread of the material. Take the ends through to the wrong side and bend them back on to fabric. Hold them in position by pinching between the thumb and forefinger of the left hand, darn in the thread and buttonhole (close blanket stitch) it on the right side along the edge. Turn on to the wrong side and darn in the thread to finish, then cut off the ends close to the stitching.

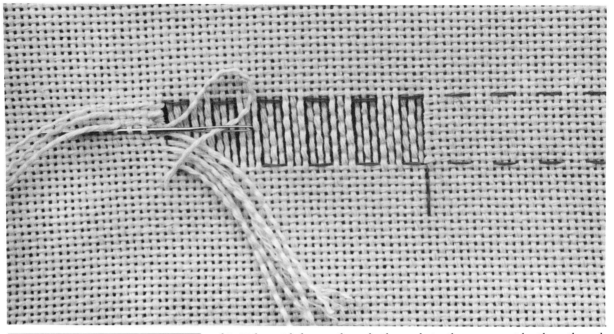

4 *Darning in ends on the wrong side*

(b) Take withdrawn threads through to the wrong side, then thread one at a time into a tapestry needle. Following the weave of the fabric, darn in the ends. To make this as invisible as possible, finish the darned ends at different lengths and cut them off close to fabric. This is a very long-winded method, but gives neat and secure results.

(c) Before removing any threads, satin stitch over a band. Withdraw the threads up to the satin stitch, and cut them off as close to the stitching as possible. The width of the band depends on the scale of the fabric. This is not as secure as the other techniques.

(d) Before removing any threads, machine a band of close zigzag across the end of the border. For extra security, work a second row on top of this, which will make a ridge. Tie off the machine ends on the wrong side. Cut withdrawn threads as close to the stitching as possible (see fig 5a).

5a *Ends secured with zigzag machining*

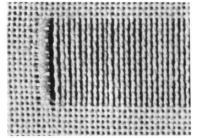
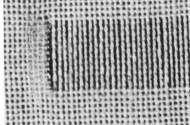

5b *Ends secured with straight stitch machining*

(e) Before removing any threads, machine three or four rows of small straight stitching very close together across the end of the border. Tie off machine ends on the wrong side. Withdraw threads and cut them close to the stitching (see fig 5b).

N.B. I find that methods (d) and (e) are neater, quicker and more secure than (a) or (c).

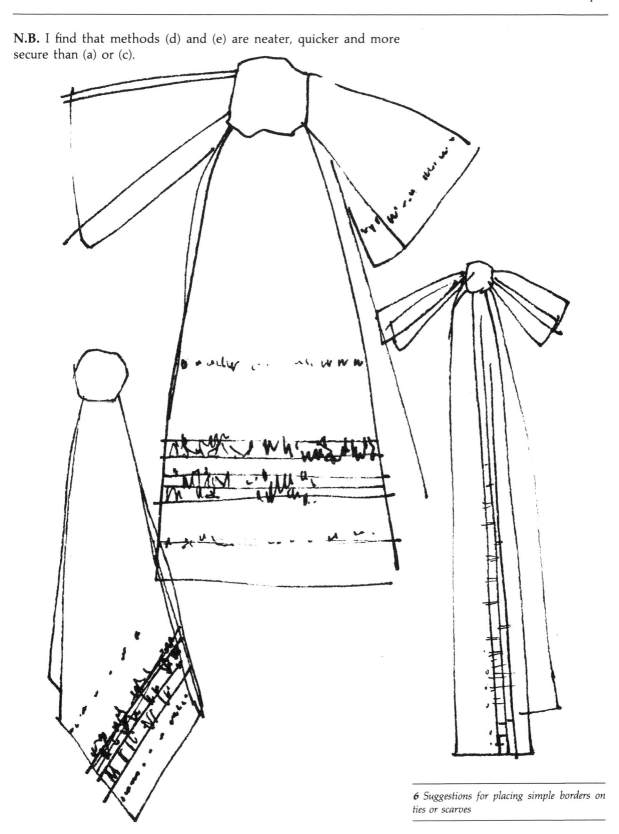

6 Suggestions for placing simple borders on ties or scarves

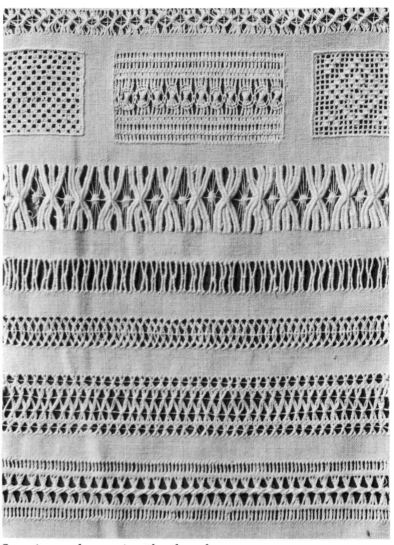

7 Part of a sampler worked by a student at the Royal School of Needlework, probably in the 1950s, showing a variety of borders and two fillings. It is on linen fabric in fine linen thread and one strand of stranded cotton (floss)

Securing and grouping the threads

It is commonly assumed that hem stitch is the only possible stitch for this purpose, but there are in fact many other stitches which can fulfil this function, and also add decorative texture. The thickness of thread is determined by the effect desired, but to use a thread of about the same thickness as one thread of the ground fabric is a good rule of thumb.

When working traditional or formal borders, first it is necessary to group the threads on either side. Use either a tapestry or ballpoint needle so that the needle passes between the threads rather than splitting them. Begin by darning in on the wrong side parallel with the border; finish by darning back into the stitchery. A back stitch made half-way along the darning-in makes it secure.

With all the stitches described here, it is necessary to pull firmly so that a clear division is made between one group of threads and its

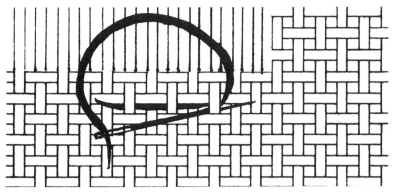

8 *Darning in on the wrong side to start the thread*

neighbour. The stitch should not lie loosely on the surface of the fabric but should be pulled in order to integrate it with the material. Because of the necessity to tension the stitching thread, the material may be more easily controlled in either a square or a round frame. If the work puckers after being worked in the hand, lay it face down on a thick pad or layers of blankets. By judicious pulling and steam ironing, it is usually not too difficult to bring it back to the desired shape.

The following selection of stitches can be used for the initial grouping, but is by no means conclusive.

● Hemstitch. This is worked in two movements and should be pulled firmly to create clear groupings. Figs 9 and 10 show three threads being counted, but the scale must be adapted to the fabric. Work from left to right.

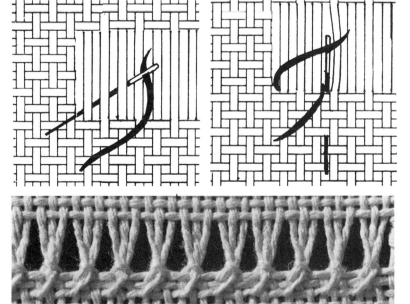

9a *First movement in hemstitch*

9b *Second movement, which completes the stitch*

10 *Hemstitch grouping threads*

17

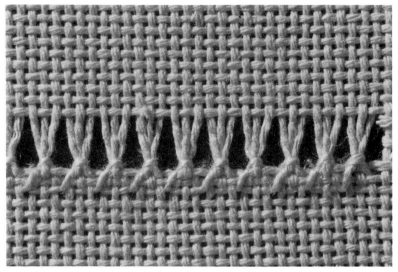

11 *Reverse of hemstitch which can also be used as the right side*

- The reverse, often used as the right side.

- Four-sided stitch. This is a pulled thread stitch in three movements: end, bottom and top stitches in that order. A cross stitch appears on the wrong side. Work from right to left.

12a,b,c *Three stages in four-sided stitch*

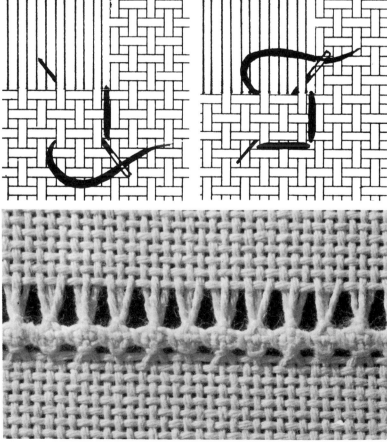

12d *Completed four-sided stitch*

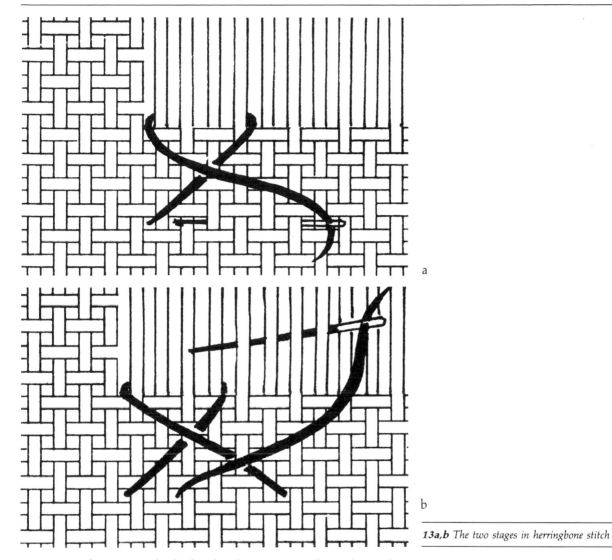

13a,b The two stages in herringbone stitch

- Herringbone extends the border decoration. Pull it tight so that the threads group, rather than being left on the surface as in surface stitchery. Work from left to right.

13c Herringbone pulled firmly to group threads

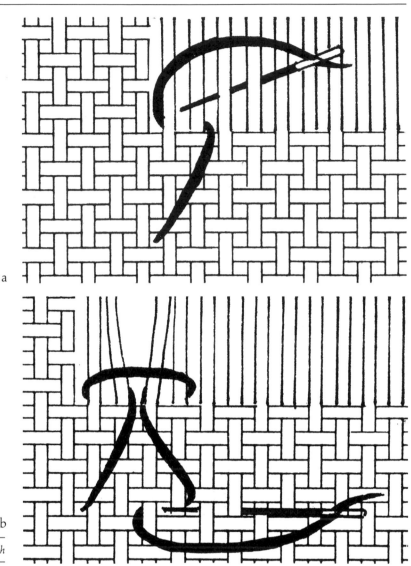

a

b

14a,b The stages of forming chevron stitch

- Chevron stitch is even more decorative than herringbone when pulled tight. Although it takes four movements to complete, it is rhythmical and pleasing to work. Use an even number of threads in each group. Work from left to right.

14c Chevron stitch makes a rich texture; pull firmly

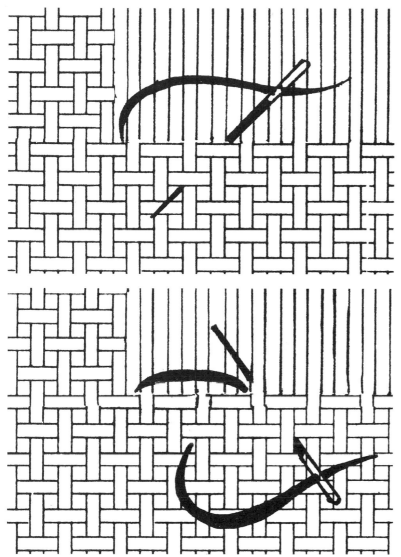

a

b

15a,b The two stages of wave stitch

• Wave stitch is another pulled thread stitch that can be used to group threads and is quick to do. Work from right to left, pulling tightly. The reverse of this stitch can also be used as the right side.

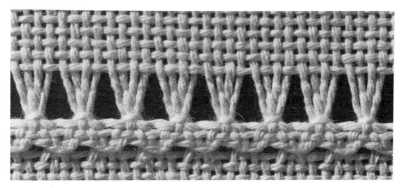

15c Completed wave stitch

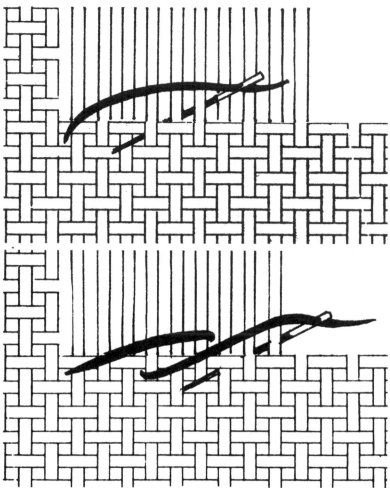

16a *How stem stitch begins*

16b *How stem stitch continues*

• A form of stem stitch was used on cloths our grandmothers and great-grandmothers embroidered. This is very much quicker than hem stitch. Thin thread about the thickness of ordinary sewing thread was often used, so that the stitch groups the threads but is more or less invisible. Work from left to right.

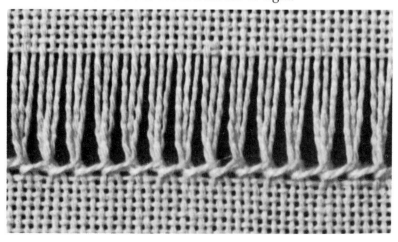

16c *Stem stitch used to group threads*

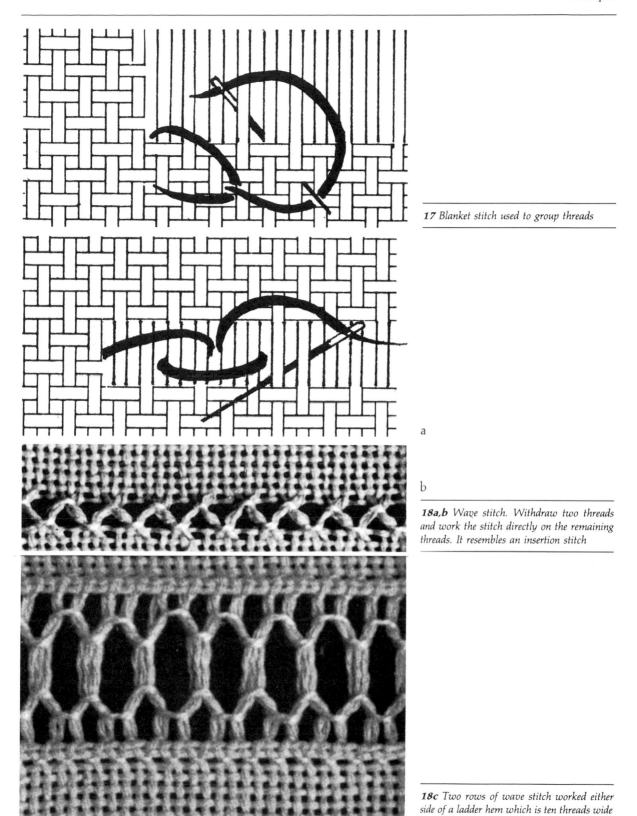

17 Blanket stitch used to group threads

a

b

18a,b Wave stitch. Withdraw two threads and work the stitch directly on the remaining threads. It resembles an insertion stitch

18c Two rows of wave stitch worked either side of a ladder hem which is ten threads wide

19 *Hemstitch worked in increasing size (over three, four, five and six threads) on evenweave linen, sewn with a ribbon-like, multicoloured knitting yarn. All the edge stitches could be varied in scale in this way to achieve a lively effect*

20 *Thick knitting ribbon on a bold fabric (cotton); both sides of hemstitch used to vary texture*

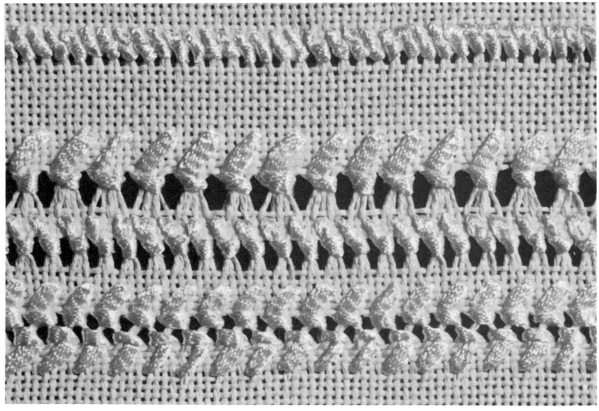

- Ladder hem. The hem stitch on either side of the border groups the same threads, forming the ladder rungs. It can be of any width but is most effective as a narrow border up to 1.5 cm ($\frac{1}{2}$ inch), depending on the scale of the fabric. This is the basis of most other kinds of decorated border when worked considerably wider.

- Zigzag hem. For this border an even number of threads must be grouped initially on one side of the border, that is 2, 4, 6, 8 etc. On the return journey along the other side, make the first stitch over half the number of grouped threads, and thereafter take half the threads from one group and half from its neighbour while hemstitching. This forms the zigzag. This works best as a narrow hem.

N.B. With all these stitches it is necessary to pull firmly so that a clear division is made between one group of threads and its neighbour. The stitch should not lie loosely on top of the fabric, but be pulled tight so that it integrates with the fabric.

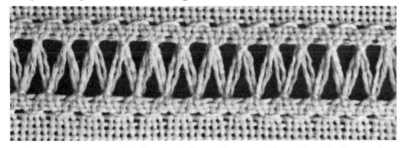

22 Zigzag hem

It is amusing to look carefully at historical work which is often assumed to be perfect; very wrongly, as it was made by people just like ourselves. It is reassuring to find errors; some drawn thread work can only be described as having cobbled edges! It seems as though the embroiderer wanted to get to the exciting bit quickly — like us! — and so withdrew the threads, bent the ends or edges back, depending on whether it was a border or filling, and then did a quick bit of oversewing in thin thread in a decidedly haphazard manner. Because the centres of the borders are exotically tied, twisted and woven, the eye is drawn to that area and so tends to overlook the uneven workmanship of the edges.

Grouping for borders

To begin, anchor the thread firmly at the end by darning in on the wrong side and taking one, or possibly two, back stitches for security. Make the needle emerge at the centre of the end.

Allow enough thread to complete the border; if it is necessary to make a join, make a weaver's knot in the thread and continue.

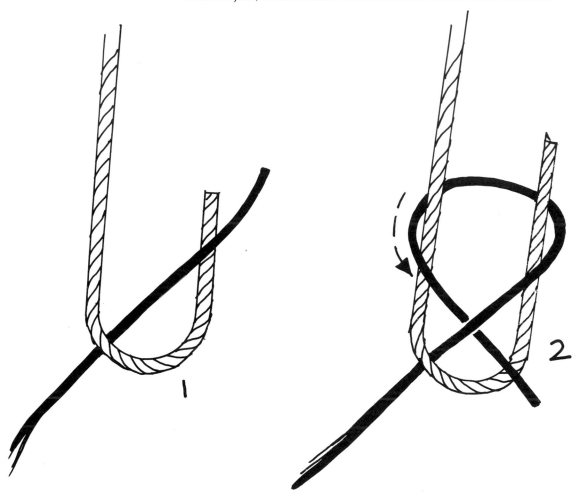

23 Weaver's knot. Intertwine threads as shown and then pull very tight. The thread may be cut very close to this knot, but it is not advisable to do this until it is integrated with the stitching

Tension is an essential part of this centre thread that controls the grouping. Either work in a frame (preferably square) or lay the work flat, on a table for example, while working.

Grouping the threads reduces the width of the border, so allow a little extra width to provide for 'shrinkage'. The bigger the bundles of grouped threads, the greater the width that needs to be allowed. Always try to use a single thread rather than a stranded one.

Tied borders

Begin this border by forming a ladder hem over a few, say two, threads. The width of the border depends on the scale of the fabric but the minimum width on a fine fabric would be about 2 cm

($\frac{3}{4}$ inch), increasing in width with the scale of the fabric. Bringing the thread through in the centre of the end, make a twisted chain stitch encompassing a group of three 'bars'.

For twisted chain stitch, place the needle on the left side of the thread before the top thread loops under it; pull really tight and it forms a knot. Continue in this fashion, ensuring that the thread lies flat and firm between each group, for maximum effect.

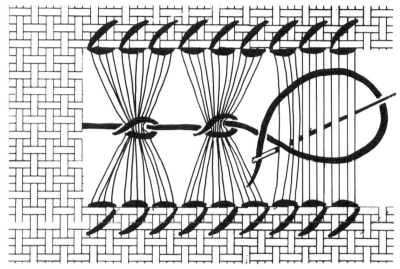

24 *Tied border*

This method of tying can be used to create all sorts of patterns in both borders and fillings.

25 *The tying on this border has been zig-zagged, taking in only two bars at a time*

Twisted borders

At first it seems that the instructions for this border are impossible and will never succeed, but if followed they do! Begin by working a ladder hem over three or four threads and about 3 cm (1¼ inch) wide on a medium-weight fabric. Bring the needle out at the centre of the end. Think of your groups as alternate 1 and 2. The needle goes under 2 and over 1 (pointing, it seems, in entirely the wrong direction). Now twist so that the needle points in the opposite direction, and magically it all becomes clear. Continue in this fashion all along the border.

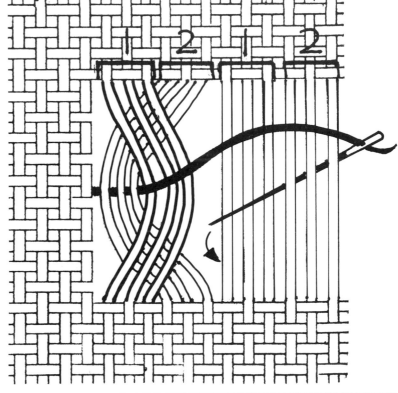

a

b

26a,b Twisted border

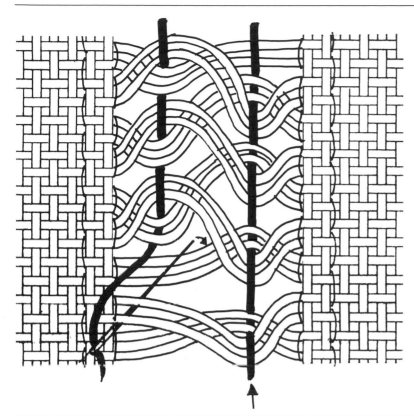

27a *Group the edge in twos; use any 'grouping' stitch such as wave, stem, etc.*

27b *Two way twist: bring the needle through at the end of the border about one third along its width; work along the border as for single twist. Fasten the thread at the end, darn and come through a little way from the other edge. Repeat the single twist in opposite direction to first line*

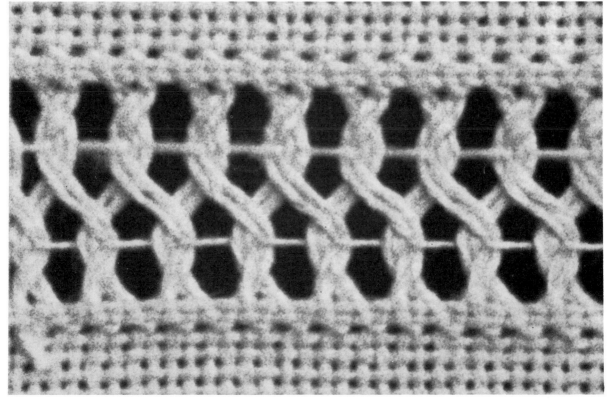

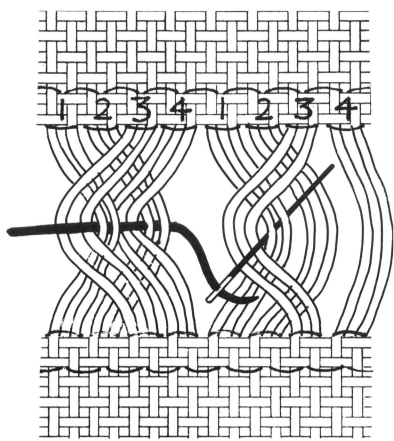

28a,b *Double twist. Group the edge in twos. Think of them as groups one, two, three and four; three twists over one and four over two. It seems impossible that it will work, but it does*

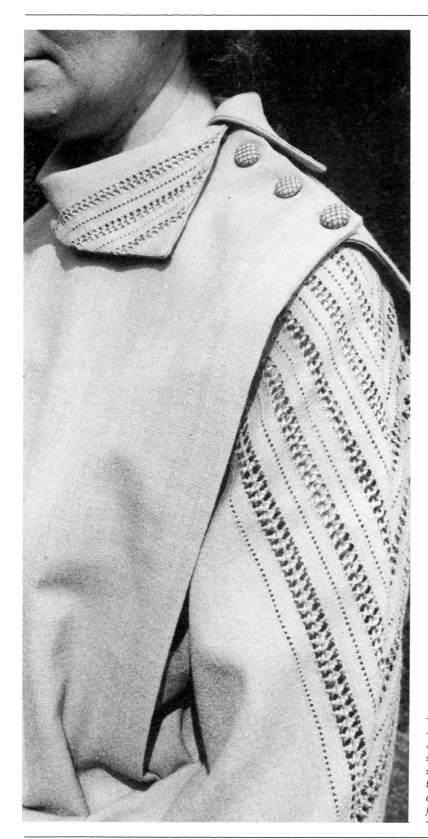

29 Detail of the decoration on a blouson top. A simple twisted border and single hem-stitched line are repeated to form texture on the sleeve and collar. It is the angle of the stitching that makes the decoration particularly interesting. Stranded cotton on grey green dress fabric (Mrs Mary Pitkethly)

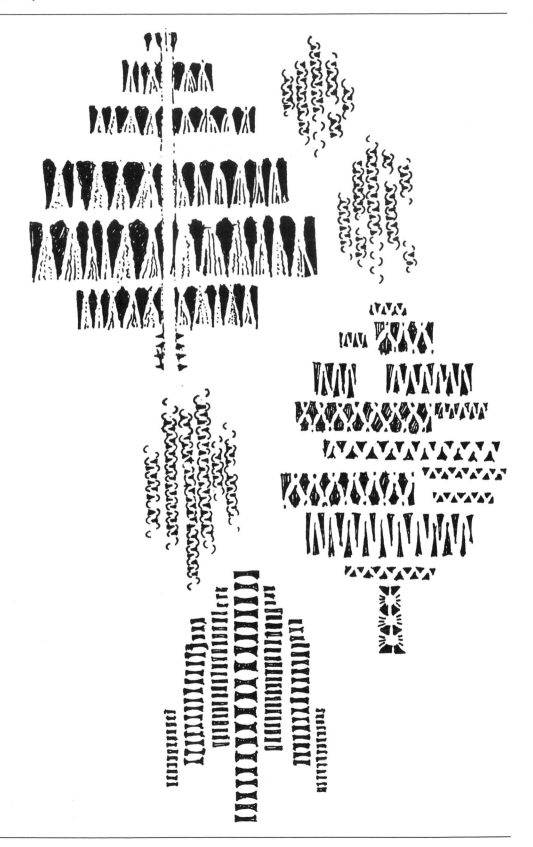

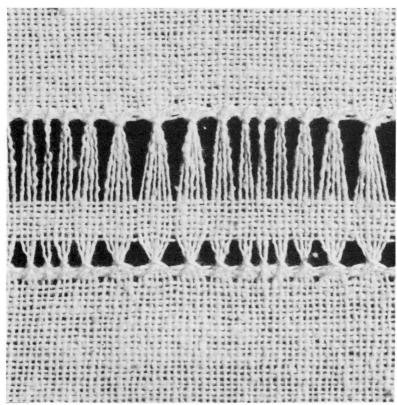

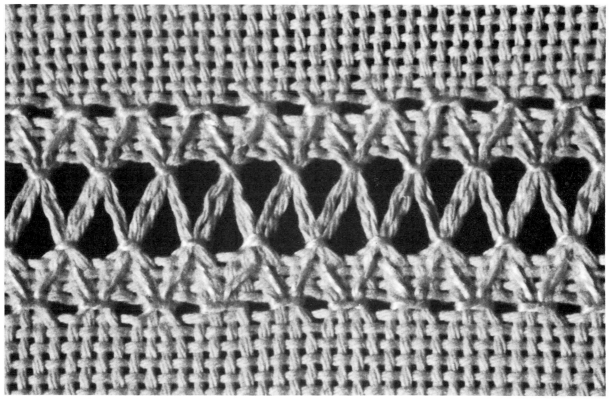

30 (opposite) Stylised trees can be formed by using borders in whole or in part, and varying the width; rows of wave stitch worked vertically can suggest bushes

31a Threads can be grouped irregularly and on one side only of a border, to give a more free effect

31b A zigzag border grouped by chevron stitch could be repeated in differing sizes and spacing to form the middle tree

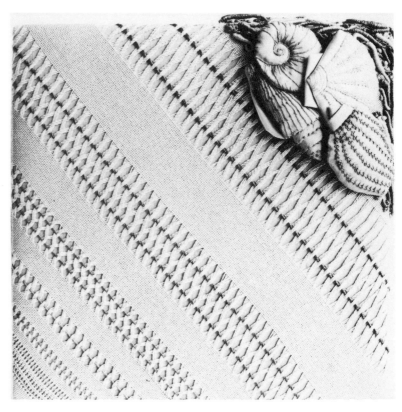

32a,b A pale green box made to a shoreline theme. Simple twist and two-way twist used in a range of sizes and mounted over sand coloured satin; surface stitched shell shapes in satin are applied at one corner (Rose Goldblatt)

Corners

When threads are withdrawn in both warp and weft to make borders, it is obvious that a hole will appear where they meet. Secure the two edges to which the threads are withdrawn, using any of the methods described on p. 17–22. The threads twisting or tying the borders are taken across the space and into the edge; this means that it must be really secure or the edge can pull out. Methods (a), (b) and (e) are the most suitable choices.

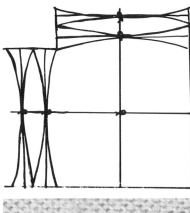 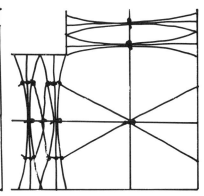 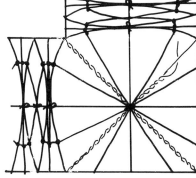

33a *Stages in constructing a corner*

33b *Finished corner*

Other threads are added to this structure using twisted chain stitch to anchor them together before being taken through the fabric. To get from one place to another, darn the thread into the edges on the wrong side or slide it through a group of threads which will hide it. It is common to make a cross with several spokes as a basis, which may then be decorated by tying and weaving, or a mixture of both.

34 *Alternative patterns for a corner incorporating weaving and tying; these need not be white but could be worked in colour on colour, for example pale blue on green*

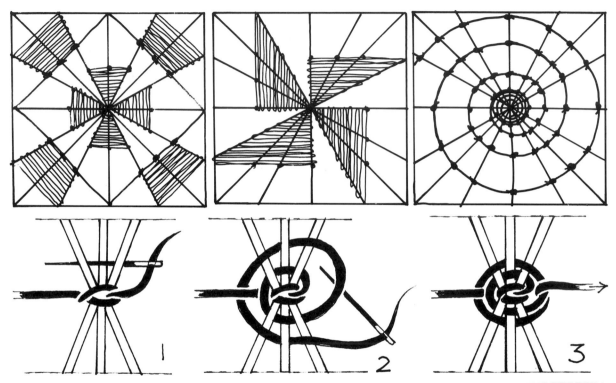

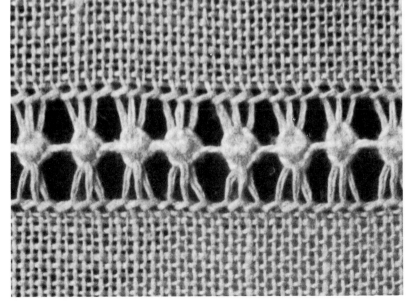

35 *Stages in making a woven border, beginning with a twisted chain stitch as in a tied border*

36 *Border with stem stitched edge and woven middle*

Weaving

Small areas of weaving, that are not what is strictly understood by needleweaving, are often incorporated with borders to make a denser area and therefore a textural contrast. These areas of weaving are worked on the threads that group tied borders, and form small rosettes or 'flowers'.

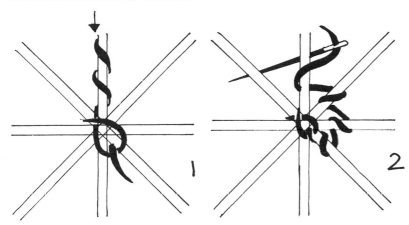

37 A spider's web may also be used for corners or borders to form a more solid area; this consists of back stitching around the fabric threads until a dense rosette is formed. Continue until the required size is made

38 Two borders, one showing a variety of options for weaving and tying and the narrower one based entirely on tying in waving lines (Gisela Banbury)

39 Stages of constructing a border. It has been assumed that the threads have already been grouped at the edge. First make a tied border (each line in the diagram represents a group of threads). Then follow 2, 3, 4 and 5 as shown. 6 is the final stage and makes a woven star; to get to the star, darn in at the edge, and wind the thread around one of the grouped threads, coming up through the centre tie before starting the weaving. Finish by darning into the weaving or taking the thread back to the edge

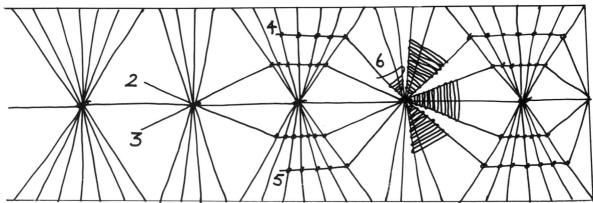

40 (opposite) A selection of borders from an old tablecloth, combining tying and weaving. By making each border different the piece is more interesting to work and to look at. Spacing borders at varying distances and making them in different widths adds to the eye appeal

41 (above), **42** (left) Spacing and widths of borders can be planned directly on fabric by using strips of newspaper. The rectangular design could be a cushion, mat or pocket; the square design a pincushion, purse or repeated on a shawl

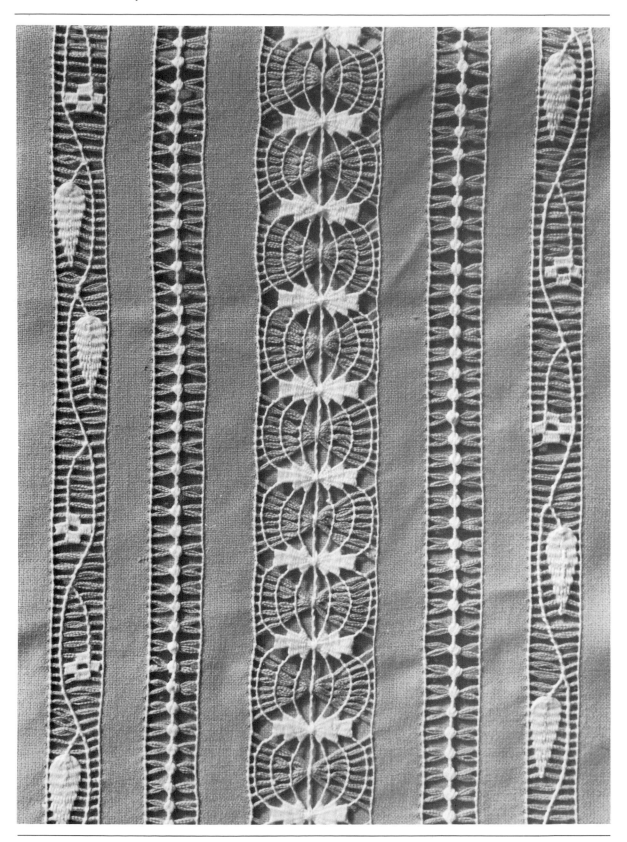

43 (opposite) *A border worked on trevira in fine pearl cotton, found in a charity shop (collection of Heather Spaulding)*

44 *Another arrangement planned in newspaper. This could be a drawstring bag or a scarf end, or inverted so that the smallest square frames a mirror. Remember that colour can be used in the fabric and the stitching, and in the backing material: for example, the thread and material could be bright jade and the backing bright pink*

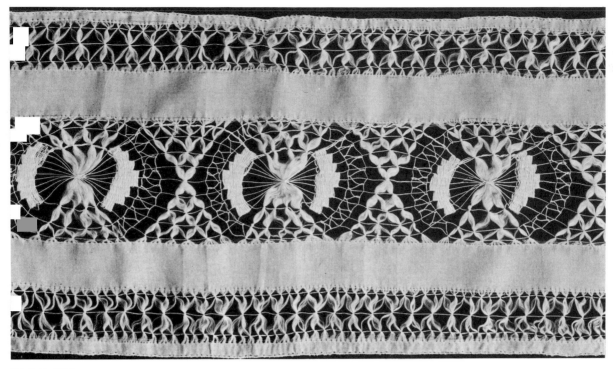

45 A border worked on fine pale blue silk, which gives a spidery, delicate look. Edwardian dresses show this form of decoration, which may have been worked in India

46 House roofs grouped together often form interesting patterns and texture. This sketch shows how such a group could be interpreted in drawn thread or drawn thread combined with pulled thread, appliqué and surface stitchery

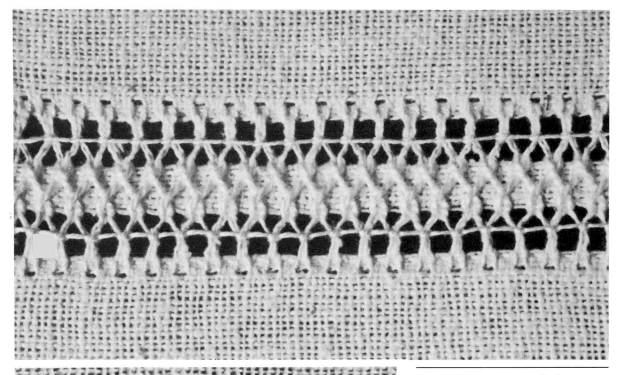

47 An adaption of a zigzag border

a

b

48a,b Two adaptions of twisted borders. Twisting the outer threads after a zigzag border has been worked, and a zigzag border grouped in fours and then each thread twisted

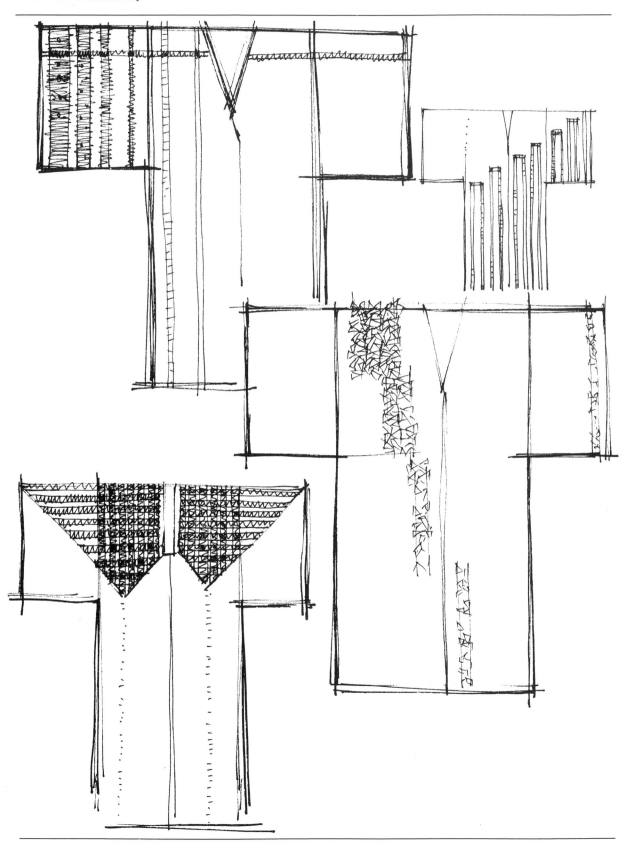

49 (opposite) Kimonos are an ideal shape for drawn thread because they are based on rectangles. A series of ideas for applying borders and fillings to the overall shape are shown

50 It is sometimes necessary to join a thread in mid border. An alternative to the weaver's knot is to turn on to the wrong side, tuck the thread under the knot (or twist) to keep it taut, and then darn it into the edge. Reverse the procedure to begin

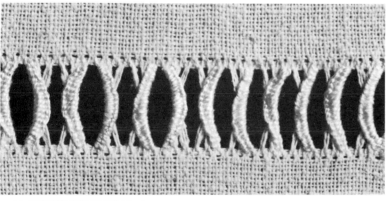

51 Buttonhole can also be used to make decoration on bars. Begin by working four buttonhole stitches over one bar, then two bars, then three bars, then reduce to two bars and one bar. Pull firmly but not tightly, and a curved bar results

52 Hessian with machine zigzagged edges; a tied border worked with a wooden bead threaded on between each tie; deep blue with yellow and orange beads

53 Tied border using knitting yarn on cotton dress fabric, letting the yarn wiggle between each stitch

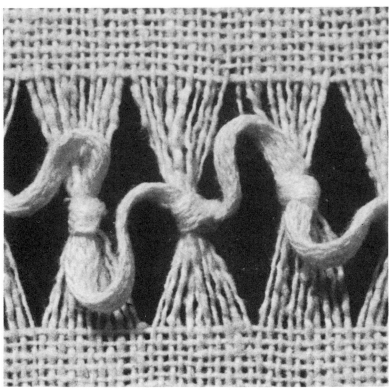

54 Ribbon worked as a tied border leaving enough length to cut diagonally between stitches

55 *Tied border using knitting yarn on dress cotton, zigzagged and then cut between stitches.*

56 *A border on dress-weight pale purple tweed incorporating drawn thread and surface stitchery. Threads used include purple, grey and mauve pearl cotton and a little silver. A raised chain band has been worked on a foundation of horizontal feather stitch, together with hemstitch and a twisted border (Christine Rapley)*

57 *A sketch of the border as it was used on a poncho-type garment from collar to cuff (Christine Rapley)*

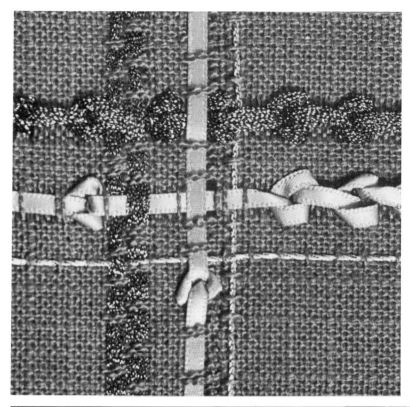

58 Raised chain band worked in ribbon and knitting yarn on withdrawn threads. By using withdrawn threads as the basic 'ladder', several composite stitches, such as raised stem stitch band, Portugese border stitch and woven band, can be worked

59 A series showing design source to finished piece. A familiar object of a plastic basket is filled with striped fabric

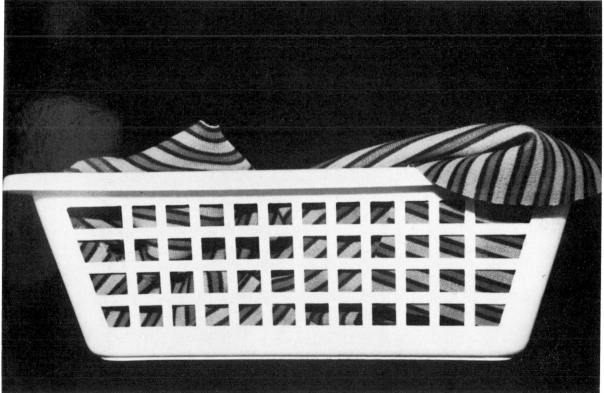

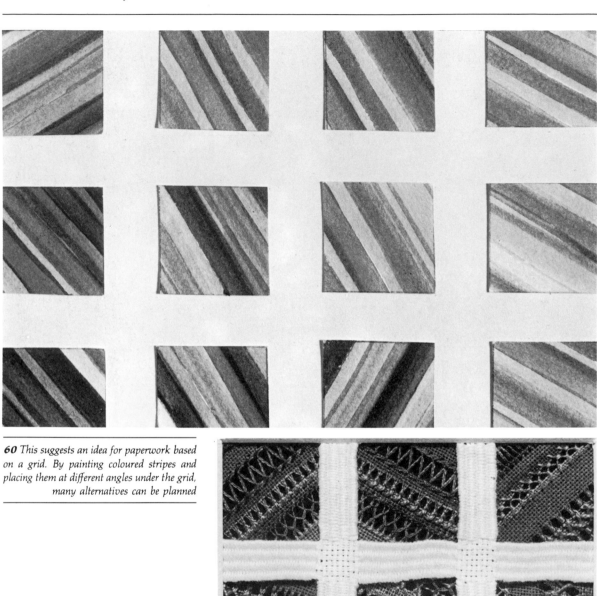

60 This suggests an idea for paperwork based on a grid. By painting coloured stripes and placing them at different angles under the grid, many alternatives can be planned

61 The final interpretation in coloured drawn thread placed under a white needlewoven grid (series by Maureen Briggs)

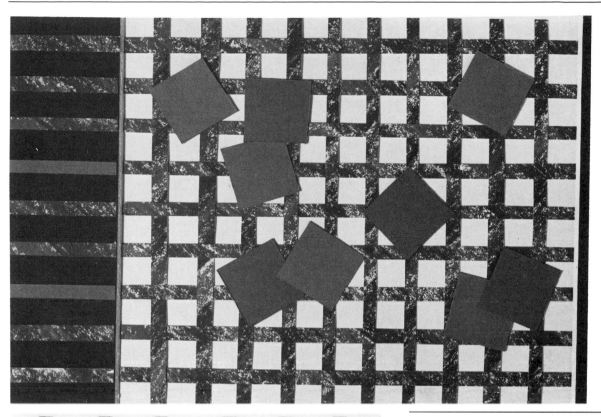

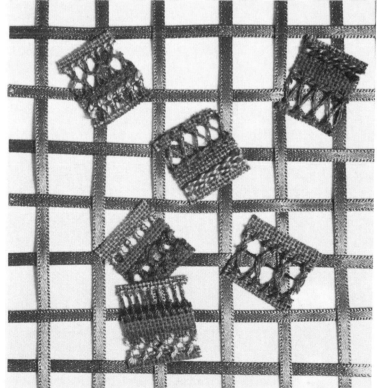

62 Another design series. In this case the grid was made of painted paper cut into strips and laid on a background. Squares of coloured paper are freely laid on top to give a lively effect (Maureen Briggs)

63 An interpretation of the design in ribbon for the grid. The coloured drawn thread borders were prevented from fraying with PVA. If the whole piece is PVAd on the wrong side, it can bleed through some fabrics, in which case only the edges should be glued before cutting; that is, glue a narrow band and allow it to dry before cutting through the middle (Maureen Briggs)

64 Another interpretation, where the background has been sprayed over square masks. Besides the drawn thread squares, several are of French knots and one of canvas or curtain net which has been coloured. The colours of this series are mainly emerald green and purple (Maureen Briggs)

Fillings

Areas of drawn thread can be worked instead of borders. Remove both warp and weft threads within an area in bands, forming a grid structure.

As before, the formal technique will be described first. As with a border, mark out the area with tacking over and under set numbers of threads for ease of counting. Cut the threads in the centre of each shape and withdraw them to the edge. The edges may be secured in any of the ways described on p. 13–15.

65 *To begin a filling. This shows the square tacked (basted) under and over four threads and the threads being cut in line with the tacking, starting at one side*

66 *Threads being cut in the opposing direction to make a grid. The edges may then be secured as for the end of borders*

The techniques of tying, twisting and weaving can be used in the same way as for borders, and may also be worked diagonally.

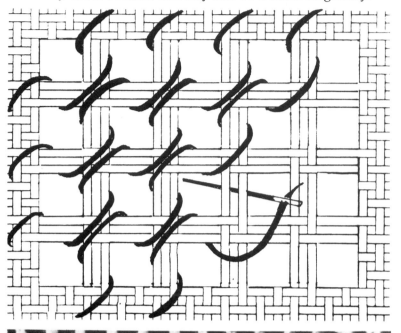

67 Filling 1. Two threads are withdrawn and two left alternately. The stitch is then worked diagonally to and fro

68 The stitch can be used solidly or can be worked on alternate rows, giving a more diagonal feel

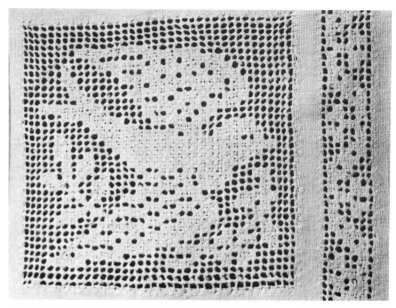

69 The whole background is worked in this filling and then the bird filled in with Greek cross. Linen thread on linen (Embroiderers' Guild Collection)

70 A shirt worked on pineapple cloth from the Philippines. Because the fabric is semi-transparent, the simple drawn thread filling has been combined with shadow work and surface stitchery (stem stitch)

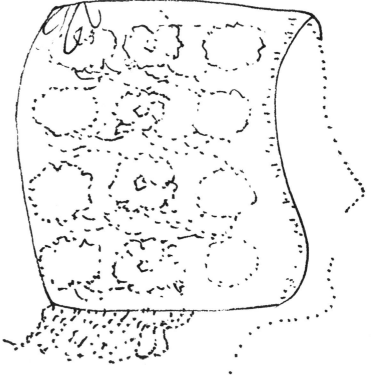

71 A stylised pansy and leaf worked in drawn and cut thread fillings in the late sixteenth century. The two motifs are repeated all over a coif. The fabric is linen, as is the thread for the fillings, but outlines are worked in chain stitch in gilt thread (Victoria and Albert Museum)

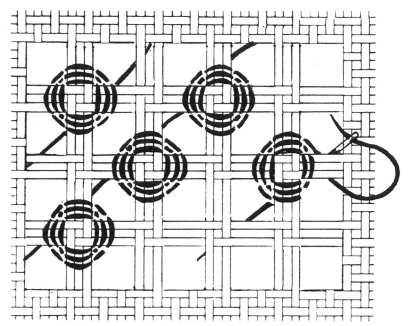

72 Filling 2. This is worked in the manner of a spider's web, backstitching around each bar. The diagram shows two threads withdrawn and two left alternately, but this could be enlarged to more threads. Working diagonally leaves a thread showing which emphasises the direction

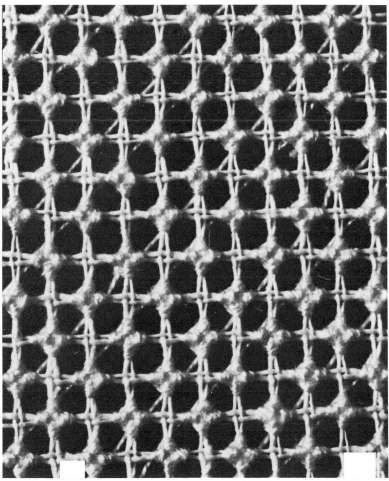

73 The completed filling looks more diamond-shaped than the diagram suggests

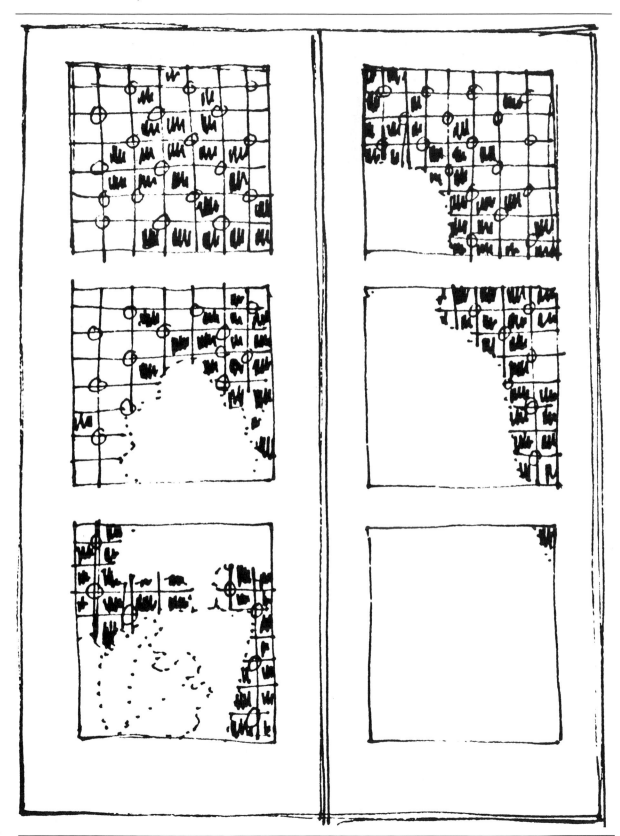

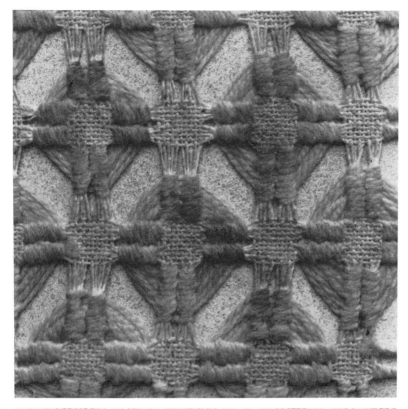

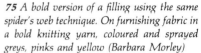

74 (opposite) This sort of filling could be used to interpret a design based on a figure silhouetted in a window. The figure could be left in plain material or surface stitched, and the window frame worked similarly to the grid on p. 57

75 A bold version of a filling using the same spider's web technique. On furnishing fabric in a bold knitting yarn, coloured and sprayed greys, pinks and yellow (Barbara Morley)

76 Filling 3. To begin, withdraw six threads and leave eight alternately. Work the horizontal lines first, twisting together first two, then four, then two of the eight threads left. Repeat, vertically knotting (p. 27) on to the horizontal threads where they cross. Work the diagonal threads in one direction, sliding under four threads of the block and under the knot. Complete the filling in the opposite direction, diagonally, weaving round the knot as you go (p. 36)

77 Buildings are a good design source for drawn thread borders or fillings, as they are based on vertical and horizontal shapes. This sketch of a building could combine several techniques such as appliqué, hemstitch, and patchwork as the 'Tudor' woodwork, with the windows as a filling

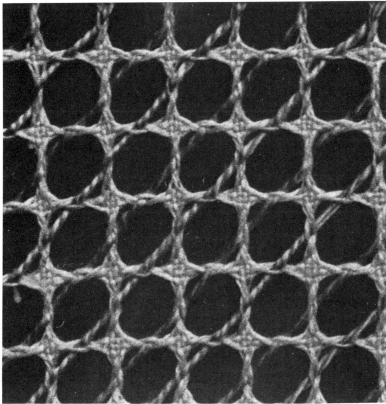

78 Filling 4. Withdraw four threads and leave four threads alternately. Working diagonally make a simple twist (p. 28) with each set of threads, that is, two over two

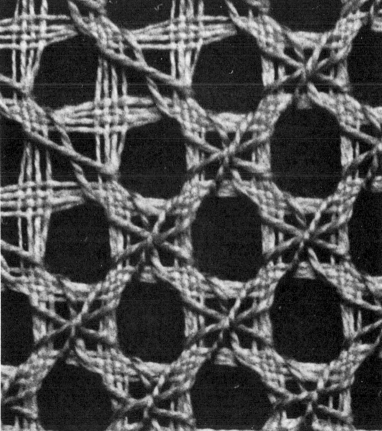

79 Filling 5. Withdraw four threads and leave four threads. This filling looks very complicated but is not. Basically it is a cross stitch worked diagonally, working half the cross stitch on the outward journey and completing it on the return journey. By repeating this in the opposite diagonal direction, a 'star' is formed. There is no reason why the filling should not be used in its half-way stage as well as complete

80 Both stages of filling 5

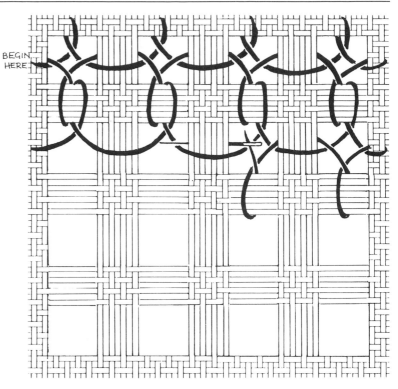

81 *Filling 6. Again this is a filling that looks very complicated but is not, as it is based on blanket stitch. Withdraw four threads and leave four threads. Begin by working a row of loose blanket stitch into the edge along one side, between each group of threads. On the return journey, alternately take a blanket stitch over four threads, then slide the thread over the previous row of blanket stitch and under four threads as shown*

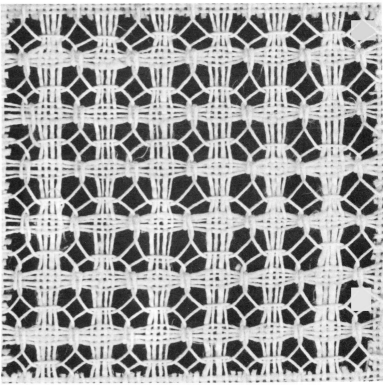

82 *The completed filling*

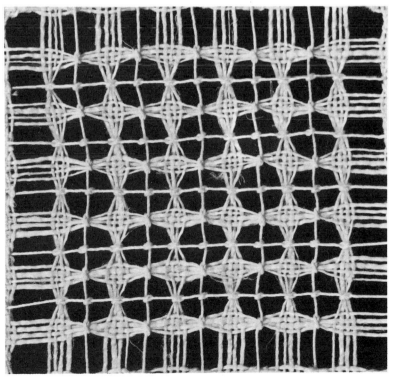

83 *Rows of urban houses like these are a very familiar sight. Because they are a collection of rectangles, they can readily be used as a design basis. Although these houses all started looking the same, their owners have altered emphasis by varying windows and doors. The same can be done in embroidery in order to avoid boring repetition*

84 *Filling 7. Withdraw four threads and leave four alternately. Work the horizontal lines first, knotting on to each group of threads. Then work identical vertical lines but knotting on to the horizontal threads as well as the groups*

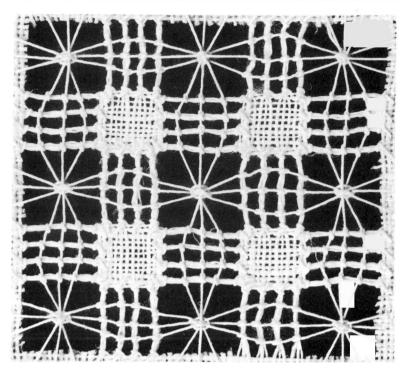

85 Filling 8. Withdraw twelve threads and leave twelve threads. Group the threads into threes by hemstitching, round the blocks and at the edge. Work three lines of stitching knotting on to the bars, between each group of threads, horizontally first and then vertically, as shown

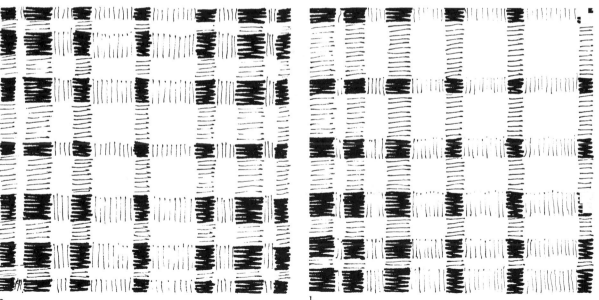

a

b

86 The fillings shown have all been counted evenly, but experiments could be made with 'irregular' counting. **a** The threads left are few at the edge, perhaps only two, and many in the middle, perhaps ten or twelve. **b** The threads left are more and more from one side to the other; as few as two threads to maybe sixteen threads

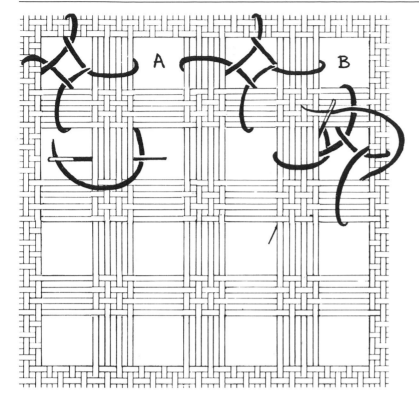

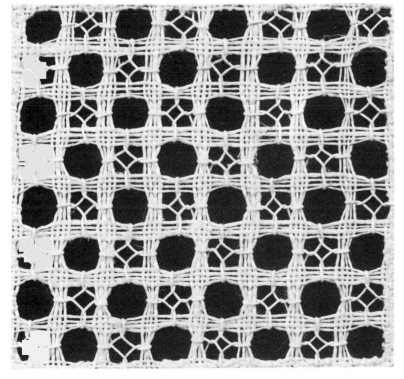

87a Filling 9. This filling is made with a Greek cross stitch. One cross is formed of four blanket stitches before moving on diagonally to the next stitch. At *A* the first stitch is shown; continue clockwise with three more blanket stitches. Tuck the thread over the first stitch as at *B* to complete the Greek cross

87b The completed Filling 9

88 A handkerchief made on very fine lawn with the edge worked in four different fillings. It was bought as a tourist souvenir in Spain in about 1958 for a few pence

89 Detail of the corners of two fine lawn handkerchieves. In a series of six, all are different. It would be interesting to know if the threads were withdrawn or whether the fabric was woven ready for the fillings. Note the way fillings are changed. From Spain, late 1950s

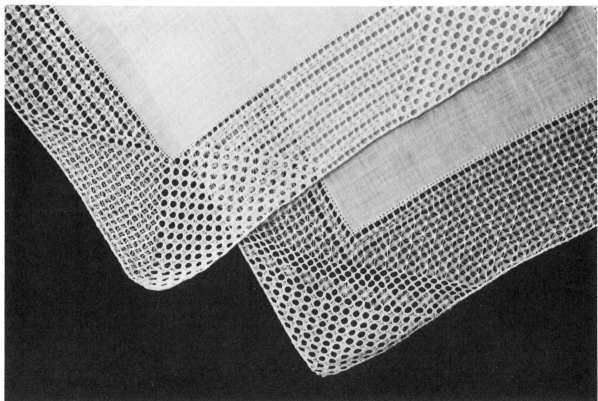

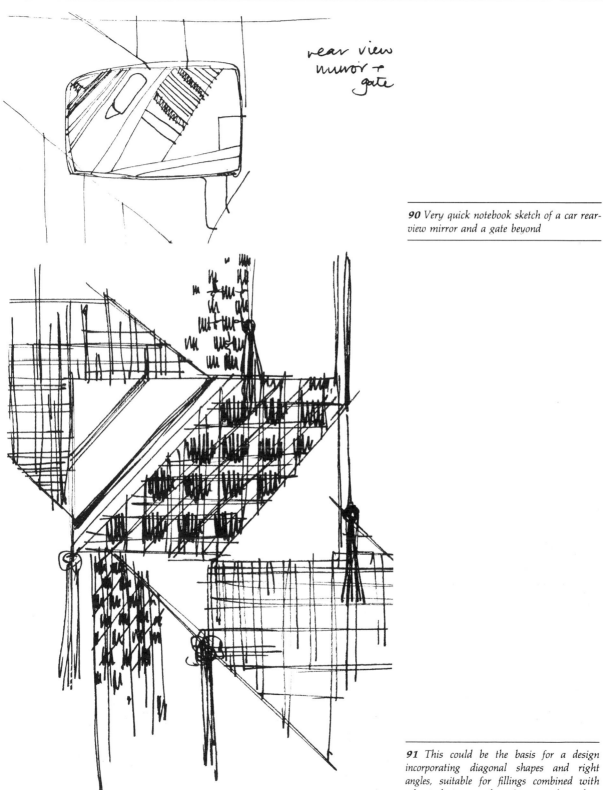

rear view mirror + gate

90 *Very quick notebook sketch of a car rear-view mirror and a gate beyond*

91 *This could be the basis for a design incorporating diagonal shapes and right angles, suitable for fillings combined with other techniques such as fringes and tassels*

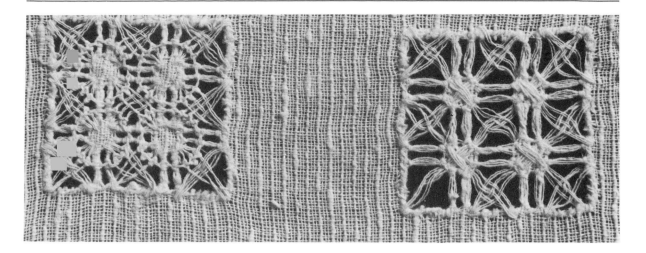

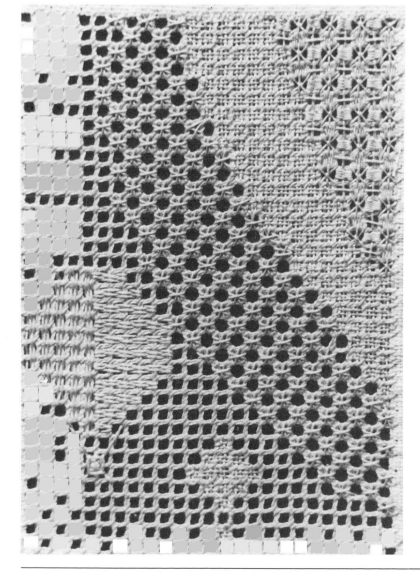

92 (opposite) A shawl made in Courtelle furnishing fabric. The design is a straightforward arrangement of borders and fillings, both appropriate to the purpose and pleasing to the eye. The fringe is secured with hemstitch, which was worked about four inches from the edge prior to the threads being withdrawn (Mrs P. D. Humphries)

93a (above) A detail of two squares from the shawl which were sewn with threads withdrawn from the fringe

93b (left) Balloons is a panel combining several fillings. It shows that they can be fitted into curved shapes. On hardanger fabric (Eileen Martin)

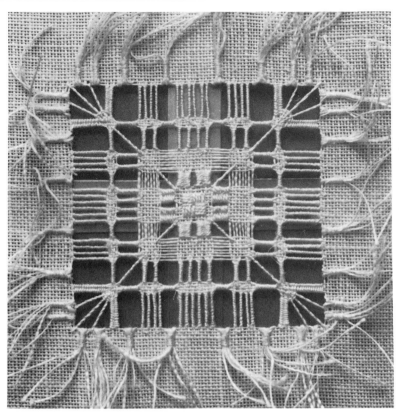

94 *A cruciform based on wrapping and weaving the threads to group them. This sort of design can be counted direct on to the fabric, and would be suitable for ecclesiastical use, for example on a burse or stole end. The threads that have been withdrawn from the filling have been bent back to be held down by blocks of satin stitches. Pearl cotton 8 and* coton à broder *on an evenweave linen*

95 *The same sort of techniques could be applied to an irregularly withdrawn square. The widths of bands of threads withdrawn and left have been randomly selected. The fabric could be space-dyed with the thread for a less formal effect, or after the stitching is complete*

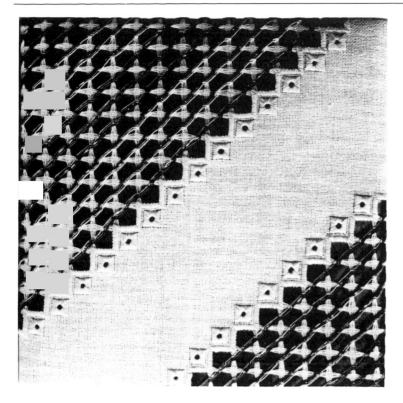

96 A box top in pale cream Glenshee evenweave with a tied diagonal filling and eyelets,
backed by deep turquoise satin. The threads
used are Marlitt, in the colourings of an
abalone shell, and pearl cotton 8 (Janet Car
lyle)

97 A view of the whole box (Janet Carlyle)

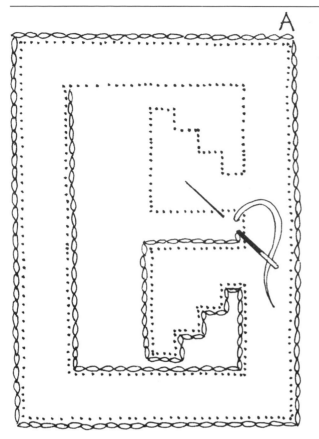

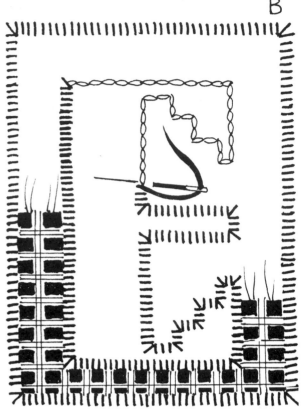

98 Russian drawn ground, Russian drawn thread, and Russian overcast filling are different names for the same technique. Like Assissi work, the background is embroidered leaving the motif in plain fabric. In (a) the preparation can be seen; the outline of the design is back stitched with a pointed needle, which acts as stay-stitching. (b) shows the next two stages; the outline of the design is satin stitched over about three threads using a tapestry needle. The threads of the material are then withdrawn in the background, withdrawing two and leaving two, and the withdrawn threads cut off as close as possible to the satin stitch after being taken through to the wrong side

99 The remaining threads are then overcast as shown, working diagonally

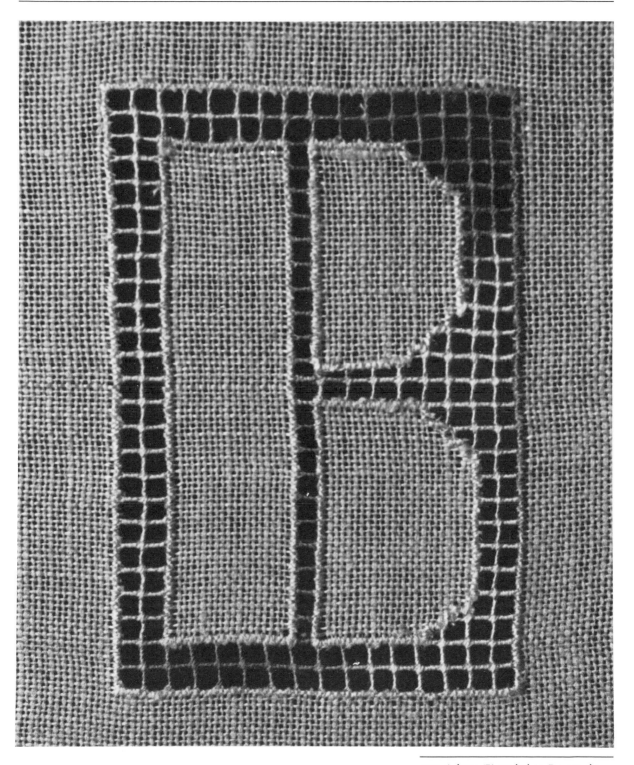

100 *A letter 'B' worked in Russian drawn ground, on pale green linen in a white to purple ombre thread (pure silk)*

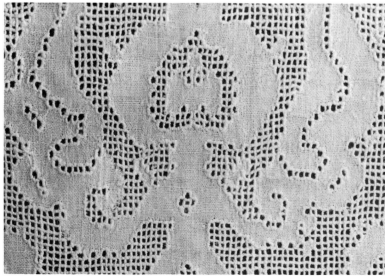

101 *A band in Russian drawn ground, linen on linen, possibly from the eighteenth century. The design clearly derives from a woven pattern, perhaps brocade (Collection of Pamela Warner)*

102 *An enlargement of a section of the band, revealing how the curves have been managed*

103a *Corner of a tablecloth, blue on white, which is a machine imitation of Russian drawn ground. There appear to be three different grid sizes, which makes the work livelier. It could be adapted for hand work. Found in a charity shop and probably dating from the mid 1930s (Collection of Heather Spaulding)*

103b *A page from a 1930s embroidery booklet showing a filling similar to Russian drawn ground, applied to lingerie*

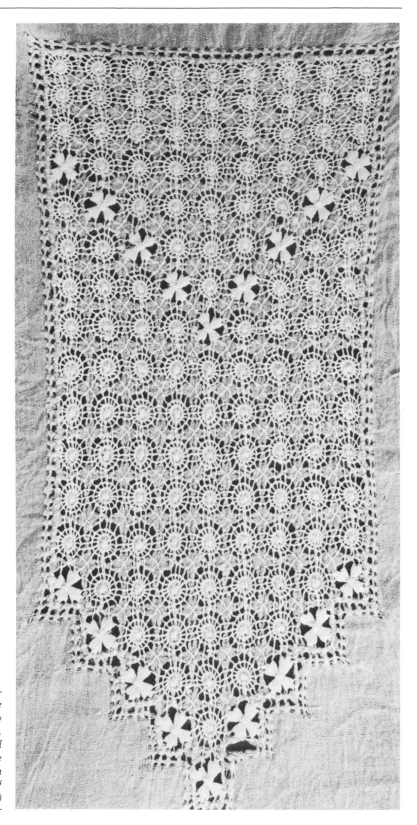

104 The end of a ceremonial scarf on pure silk. The shape and decoration could fit equally well into the yoke of a dress or a small bag, when the filling could be worked in metal thread. The 'V' in woven crosses is an effective visual surprise and textural contrast, which adds life to the overall pattern (Collection of Pamela Warner)

105 An enlargement showing the intricacy of the filling based on vertical, horizontal and diagonal tying

Modern extensions of drawn thread borders and fillings

Nowadays few people have the time or inclination to work large areas of drawn thread in regular patterns. There are therefore modern alternatives for working.

- Why must all the grouping be regular? Experiment with varied grouping, that is by going over 2, 4, 6 and 8 threads in order, and then perhaps diminishing in the same order. Alternatively, grouping could be entirely random

- Need the work always be in white or monochrome? Rich coloured fabrics may be used, for example emerald sewn with bright cerise. Or fabrics and threads may be space- or rainbow-dyed, which breaks up the feeling of symmetry

- Yarns other than embroidery threads can be used, for example ribbons, strips of fabric or thongs of leather. This makes the formal tying or twisting look quite different

- Metal threads suitable for sewing or machining, such as knitting yarns and machine sewing threads, can be used. These can enrich the work, making it look jewel-like, and precious

- Beads of all kinds can be incorporated in drawn thread. They can be threaded on between tying stitches, or incorporated in weaving

- Experiment by *not* working a grouping stitch either side of the 'border', rather just tying, twisting or weaving the threads, grouping them by eye or randomly.

106 *A photograph of a street scene with lamp-post is photocopied; the photocopy is then cut into strips and mounted on a black background, forming an altered and simplified version of the original photograph to create a design (Vicki Hinton)*

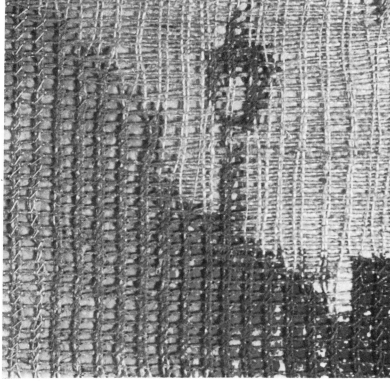

107 *A free interpretation of the design on hessian: threads have been withdrawn and those remaining freely sewn. Both the fabric and background have been colour printed with the simplified street scene (Vicki Hinton)*

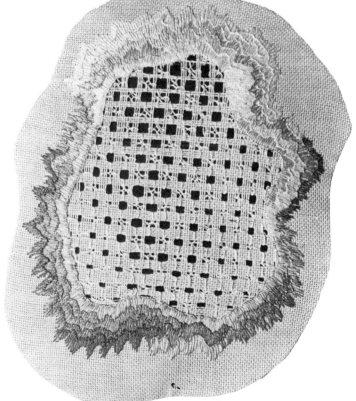

108a A box top to the theme of 'shoreline'. The whole fabric top has been covered with blocks of satin stitch over a withdrawn grid; on top of this has been added a shell in surface stitchery incorporating a stone, and seaweed in needleweaving (Ena Gibson)

108b The whole box which is in terracotta lugano fabric, embroidered using pearl cotton 5 and 8 (Ena Gibson)

109 Random shaper, secured round the edge by rows of buttonhole stitch in shaded thread. Filling 9 has then been worked on irregularly drawn threads, giving a shaded effect (Pamela Pavitt)

3 Hedebo

Hedebo embroidery comprises a range of cut and drawn techniques. The agreed facts are that the linen fabric was grown and handwoven in a heathland area of Denmark. It was then embroidered by the peasant women, white on white, to decorate their homes as hangings, friezes over the bedstead and decorative towel ends, and was not necessarily meant for practical use. It has always been rich in texture, contrasting bold and rich surface stitchery with open areas. The open areas in early work, made in the first half of the nineteenth century, appear to be drawn thread, whereas thereafter shapes were cut out of the fabric, edged with a particular buttonhole stitch with a knotted edge, and filled with needlelace patterns.

A point of common ground is that the designs were not necessarily geometric and contained stylized floral shapes. Early work shows some of the negative, or background, areas being worked, whereas later Hedebo embroideries show motifs of elaborate eyelets while the background is richly surface stitched.

The main point of interest is that in earlier work the drawn thread fillings were contained in flowing shapes, not squares or rectangles.

The technique needs to be worked on a closely woven fabric; using a pointed (crewel) needle work three rows of close chain stitch around the edge with a single thread such as pearl coton 12 or *coton à broder*. When this is complete, withdraw the threads up to this stitching and then cut them off close to it on the wrong side to form a basis for the filling.

In modern work the rows of enclosing chain stitch could be in threads of varying thickness, or more rows added. Chain stitch is not the only stitch that can be used: stem stitch, split stitch, overlapping herringbone and many other 'line' stitches are equally appropriate if they integrate well with the fabric. Machine stitching, whether it be close rows of straight stitch, zigzag, or a mixture of both, offers new possibilities.

110 *A quick sketch of a truss of tomatoes. If a sketch is made in felt-tip there is no chance to change your mind. Do not worry if it is not a complete, accurate representation of the real shapes, as it has to be adapted to form a design*

111 *Using the tomato sketch as an idea. It has been simplified to make shapes suitable for this piece of a modern version of hedebo. The tomatoes are outlined with chain stitch in varying numbers of rows before drawn thread fillings are worked. The stem is buttonholed over a thick thread. Pearl cotton 8 and coton à broder on linen*

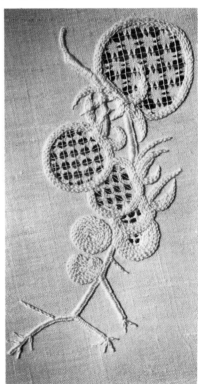

4 Needleweaving

Weaving or darning with a needle may well have been one of the earliest forms of embroidery. It is sometimes difficult to decide whether some of the very early patterning in Egyptian textiles was woven or needlemade. In more recent times, during the past two hundred years or so, areas of geometric needleweaving in colour or white have been combined with other counted thread stitchery to form richly patterned areas on peasant dress and house furnishings. This kind of decoration can be seen in many countries, including Eastern Europe, Russia and Turkey.

In England in the seventeenth century, when samplers were records of patterns and stitchery, many showed bands of needle-weaving and reticella. In general these drawn thread techniques are worked in monochrome, but they are frequently combined with coloured counted thread borders and units of design in cross stitch, satin stitch and double running stitch. The ground fabric is invariably linen with reticella and needleweaving worked in linen thread, but occasionally a free thinking embroiderer has worked a section in coloured silks. One such sampler is in the Goodhart Collection at Montacute in Somerset, and dates from the mid to late seventeenth century. There are five bands in monochrome and a little decorous colour in the two mermaids in the sixth, but in the seventh and last bands the embroiderer has really enjoyed herself. The design shows a man and woman; a fountain with foliage and a few small birds fill the rest of the reticella grid. What is unusual is that the work is entirely in colour, with some metal thread, and one bird still has a bead eye.

During the past hundred years in Britain directions for working needleweaving have appeared from time to time in women's magazines; a *Needlewoman Embroidery* booklet of the 1920s illus- trates a runner and the 1930 and 1931 issues of the *Embroideress* illustrate a cushion and an all-over design that can be adapted for a bag and a cushion. The designs are invariably in simple blocks of contrasting colour, intended for decorating items of dress or household use.

The present understanding of formal needleweaving is that the

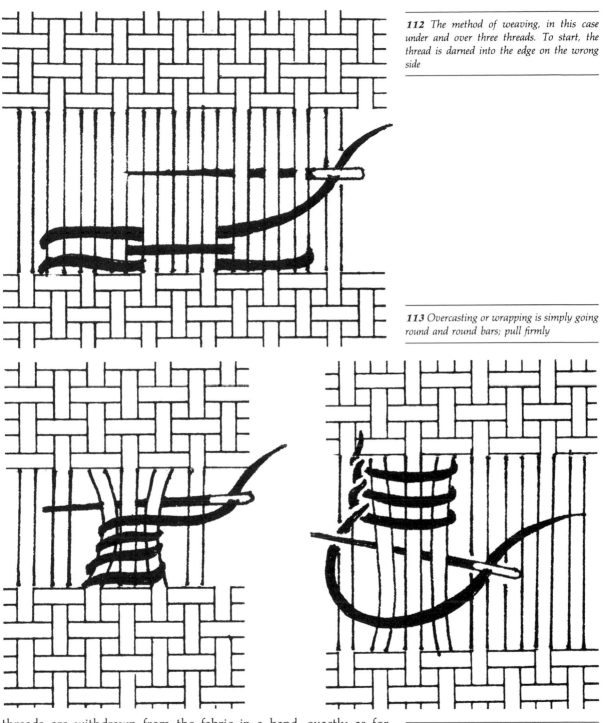

112 The method of weaving, in this case under and over three threads. To start, the thread is darned into the edge on the wrong side

113 Overcasting or wrapping is simply going round and round bars; pull firmly

114 Buttonhole can also be used to cover bars; it tends to twist around the bar which can be used effectively. Push stitches close together, but do not crush them in or the bar will stretch and wiggle

threads are withdrawn from the fabric in a band, exactly as for drawn thread borders; a geometric border is then formed by weaving under and over regular counted groups of threads.

For many patterns it is not necessary to group the threads first by stitching the edge, as the weaving itself does the grouping. The permutations of patterning in this way are infinite, even with such a limited stitch movement. Weaving may also be allied with threads which are overcast, wrapped or buttonholed.

115 A series of needlewoven borders showing that the edges need not be grouped. The bottom border has been worked using two thicknesses of thread

116 More needlewoven borders. In the top one the threads have been grouped with wave stitch, and on the bottom one two thicknesses of thread have been employed; pearl cotton 5 for the weaving, and pearl cotton 8 for the overcasting

If only one colour is used, variation can be achieved by altering the thread thickness. Stitching woven blocks in contrasting colours, for example, red, jade and cerise, on a white ground, achieves a bold

117 Showing how dark, medium and light toned colours can be used to emphasise the pattern in needleweaving; for example, three tones of green, dark, mid-green and pale green; or yellow, red and navy blue

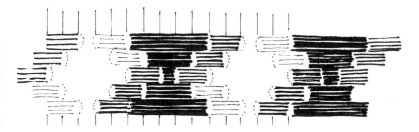

peasant-like effect. Alternatively, coloured fabric may be used and contrasting colours worked into it.

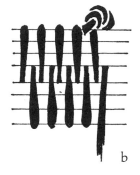

118a,b Bullion picot. Wind the thread around the needle three times, firmly but not tightly. Hold this winding between thumb and forefinger while pulling the needle through. Ease to required position and continue weaving

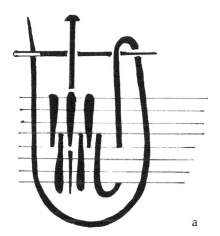
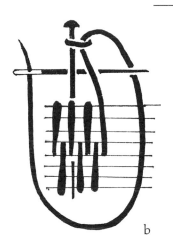

119a,b,c Place a pin in the weaving, and take a stitch to encompass the pin as shown in (a); this is the same as tying in a tied border. Ease the stitch a little way up the pin and work three buttonhole stitches back to the weaving, see (b) and (c). Picots make little knobs that can alter the texture on weaving

120 A series of window-like blocks of needleweaving, altering the grid proportions each time. The white hardanger fabric has been sponged with red and yellow and a touch of mauve paint, and the needleweaving has been worked in matching colours (Margaret Walker)

Needleweaving may be worked on any fabric from which threads may be withdrawn, whether coarse or fine. Fabrics such as velvet, which may initially seem quite unsuitable, can give particularly effective results, as the needlewoven band lies below the level of the pile.

It is easiest to work with a single thread. Choose from those mentioned on p. 11. The most suitable are pearl cotton in its various thicknesses, *coton à broder*, soft embroidery cotton (*retors à broder*) and buttonhole twist. Experiment with woollen yarns, crochet cottons, string, ribbons and fabric strips, as these can give lively and interesting textures.

It is wise to use a blunt needle, either tapestry or ballpoint, as this prevents snagging the ground material.

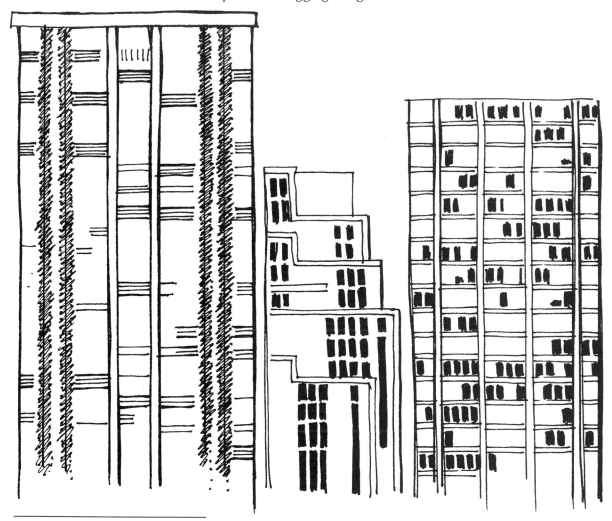

121 At first sight, tower blocks are very uninteresting rectangles; but on closer inspection curtains or blinds, pulled or not pulled, make a random pattern within the shape and liven it up. The same idea can be developed in interpreting these buildings; visual irregularity catches the eye

122 Section of a photograph of New York

123 A photocopy of the photograph, which simplifies the overall shapes and emphasises the irregular window pattern in the tower block

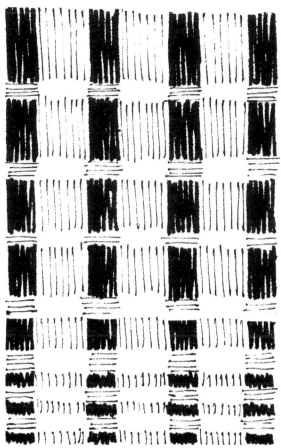

124 A grid based on lines getting closer towards one end, which can suggest perspective

125 Weaving ribbons simply between withdrawn threads can create patterns. Grey and silver ribbon on a mixed green/mauve dress fabric

126 This is the reverse of the woven ribbon sample in Fig 125; it can be seen how the ends are held with machining

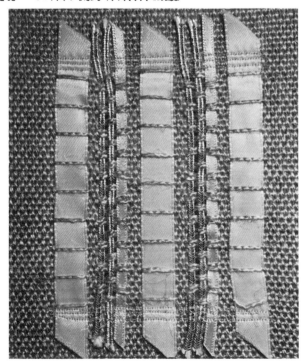

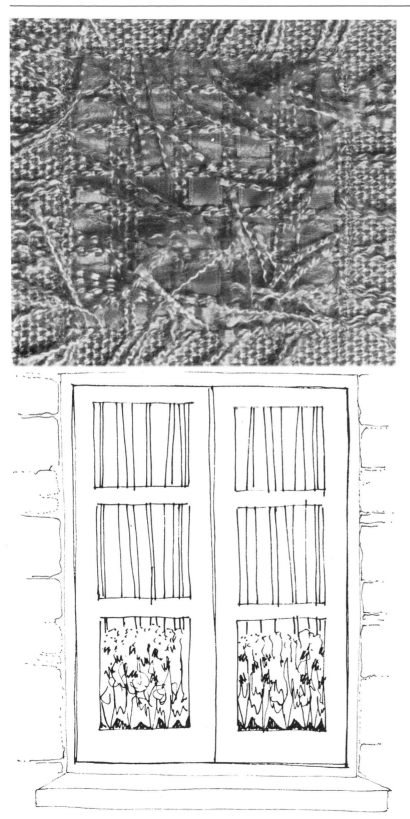

127 (above) In this case leather strips and thick woollen yarn have been woven into blue hessian

128 (top left) Ribbon woven into fabric. The withdrawn ends of fabric have not been cut off, but have been machined so that they go every way

129 Sketch of a curtained window. The curtains could be worked in the techniques shown, with the window frame of padded fabric overlying them. Walls and sill could be worked in machine stitchery, in straight stitch for the stone and zigzag for the sill and outer frame

The formal technique may well be too rigid for modern designs, but there is no reason why it should not be worked freely, as it lends itself readily to this style of working. Begin with a design source that suggests appropriate shapes, such as a stand of trees in winter, a bare hedgerow, or ripples on water. Remove threads from the fabric within the shape, finishing them off at the edge in any of the ways mentioned on p. 13–14. Using weaving, overcasting or button-holing, group the threads in an irregular fashion, making some areas dense and others spidery and open; refer to the shapes in your design source but do not copy them slavishly. Vary the thread thickness within one area to make further textural variation. Vary the tension of the stitching to make some parts of the design tightly controlled and others more open.

130 Sketch of a plant form in the garden

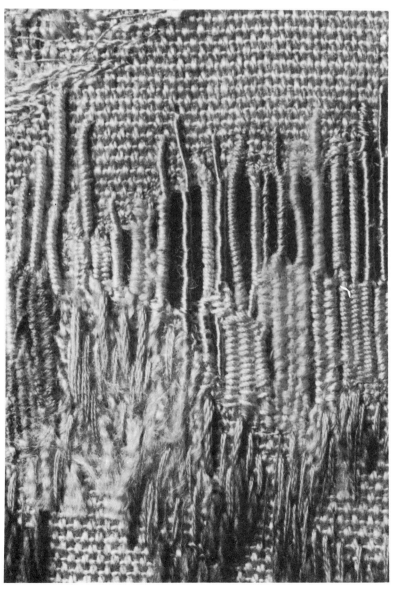

131 Free use of wrapping and weaving in many different threads to suggest a flower border, which is linked to the fabric with free straight stitching. 'Flowers' are in pinks and mauves, and straight stitching in the same colours and greens, on a greeny dress fabric

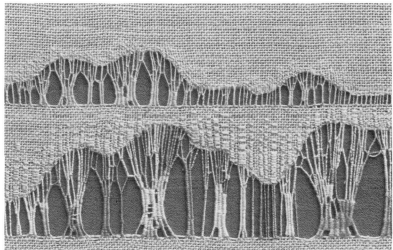

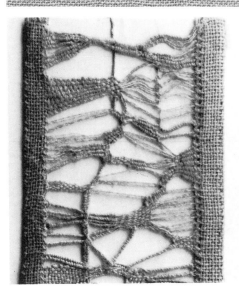

132 Quick sketch of trees in winter

133 Winter. *A panel based on tree forms in winter; the wavy shape at the top is secured with small straight machine stitches, the threads withdrawn and held back with straight stitching by hand to suggest the furrows in a field. Mainly in ombre pure silk thread, green and khaki to cream, on a pale green fabric*

134 *Random needleweaving can be great fun, especially for those people who find regular counting onerous. On a woollen fabric in self threads (Miss Hockerday)*

135 *More random stitching in buttonhole and overcasting, working across three withdrawn bands*

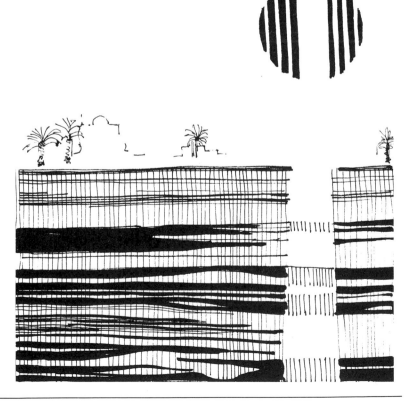

136 *A design derived from a photograph showing sun or moon over sea. The sea would readily translate into free needleweaving*

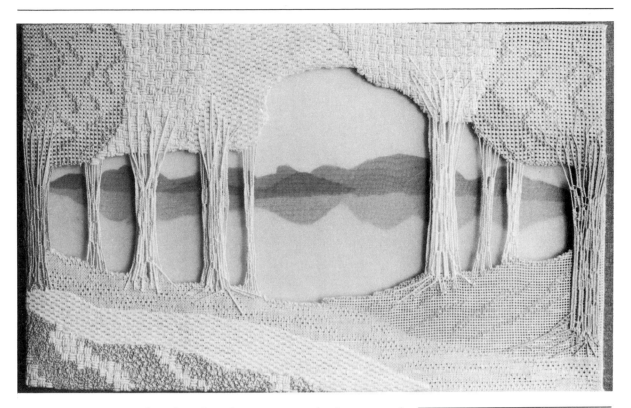

Removing every other thread within an area in both warp and weft, means that two layers of threads will emerge at right angles to each other. These can be embroidered separately to give a layered effect.

Ukranian openwork

This is a form of needleweaving employing quite a different technique, mentioned in older publications. It is a form of mass-production needleweaving, and is quick and effective to do, as it is basically a kind of couching.

The method is to remove four threads, then leave four in a band perhaps eighty threads wide. The design may then be marked on the band with tacking (basting) or a water-soluble pen. Blocks of stitching are then worked between the design lines, the different areas of the design being filled with different colours. Because the stitching is so well integrated with the fabric, Ukranian openwork is particularly suitable for practical items, such as clothing.

137 A very richly textured embroidery of trees with water and mountains beyond. The trees have needlewoven trunks, with other areas in pulled thread, rose point and surface stitchery. The mountains are suggested with layered transparent fabrics (Mrs Dickens)

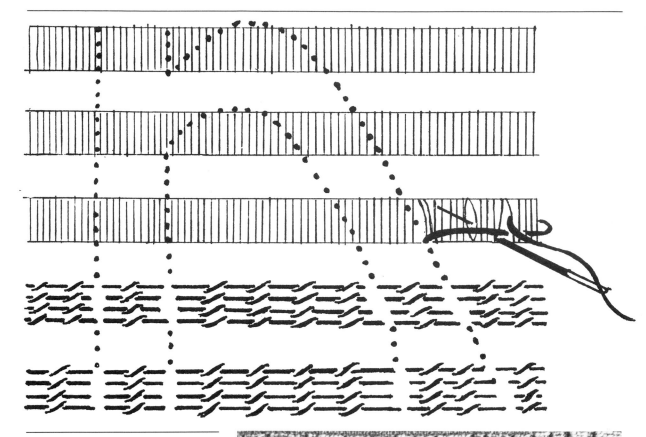

138 Stages in Ukranian openwork, showing the withdrawn bands, the outline design of an 'n' and the stitch being worked

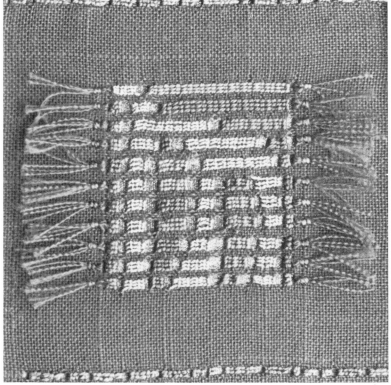

139 A finished piece of Ukranian openwork based on the letter 'm'. In jades and blues on a cerise moygashel fabric, mounted over silver

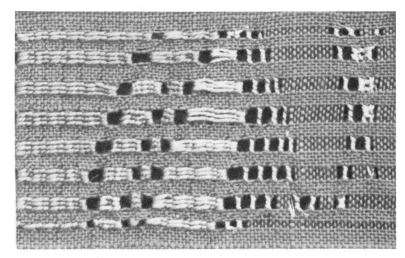

140 *Using the technique more freely*

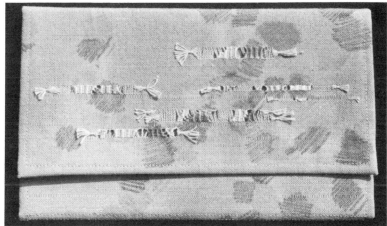

141 *A pochette bag with bands of free Ukranian openwork linked in colour to the ground fabric, which has been coloured in felt-tipped blobs*

142 *Textile jewellery, bracelets, a necklace and a choker, made from wrapped and needlewoven binca material. The colours in the embroidery are blue, red and yellow with black, making it very dramatic. The binca is completely covered with stranded cotton (floss) and pearl cotton (Valerie Riley)*

5 Reticella

Reticella is a complex construction of stitchery, yet appears to be one of the earliest forms of drawn thread. It looks like lace and was in its prime when the first simple bobbin lace of plaited bars was still at a very elementary stage. Basically, the method is to withdraw almost all the thread from a fabric, leaving only a skeletal grid structure, and then refill the spaces with elaborate geometric patterns based on laid-in bars.

Because painters in the sixteenth and seventeenth centuries were so accurate in their detail, we are indebted to them for being able to see exactly what reticella looked like and how it was used. Portraits of the most fashionable members of late sixteenth and early seventeenth century society show examples of collars, ruffs and cuffs in excellent detail. The fashion for this form of embroidery on these items spread through Western Europe, and collar decoration varied depending on the prevailing fashion. The ruff could be a flowing large or small figure eight or pleated and angular, and was often decorated with lacy embroidery along its outer edge. An overall length of nine yards of fabric was needed for the most extravagant mill ruffs. Reticella is more frequently seen in standing collars, however; these were collars worn by both sexes, sometimes closed at the neck and sometimes, on female dress, rising from either side of a square neckline to make a very fetching frame for the face. Collars of all sorts were stiffly starched, and there was at one time a fashion for colouring starch. Standing collars had to be supported by a wire framework, called a *supportasse*.

Men gradually had their hair cut shorter to accommodate the size of standing collars as they developed from a small wing to cover a much larger area. These dramatic collars frequently had matching cuffs, and the rest of the ensemble was richly textured with embroidery and slashing.

Clothing in those days was in many different pieces – that is, the sleeves were separate from the bodice, which in turn was separate from the skirt, underskirt and shift – so that there were many options in the mix and match selection of clothing. It also meant that it took some time to dress as buttons were uncommon, while

ties and pins were more frequently used. As collars and cuffs needed to be seen from both sides, the embroidery had to be reversible (as, indeed, double running patterns for cuffs had to be half a century earlier).

Most patterns were geometric because of the basic grid, that is, it was divided into stars and 'snowflake' patterns. In the 1604 pattern book *Newes Modelbuch* by Hans Siebmacher, the majority of the 37 extant plates are based on grids of various sizes, some appropriate for canvas work but many clearly intended for reticella, even to the knobs for picots. There are many variations on the snowflake theme and on one page as many as nine alternatives of square designs with semi-circular additions are shown. These designs are clearly illustrated in the standing collars and cuffs as seen in Henry Bone's enamel of Lady Manners at Kingston Lacy, Dòrset, in a miniature of

143 A drawing based on the miniature of a young man from the early seventeenth century. The standing collar he is wearing clearly illustrates reticella, and frames his handsome face very becomingly

a

b

144a,b *Two patterns from the Newes Modelbuch of Johann Siebmacher (1604). There are in the book many patterns like (a), showing the square reticella motif, attached to the semi-circular motif to be made in needle-lace, and which, when repeated, are obviously the bases for the standing collar borders, and other articles of dress. There is also a great similarity between (b), and other patterns like it, to those worked on samplers later on in the same century*

Richard Boyle, Earl of Cork, at the National Portrait Gallery, and in a portrait of Susanna Temple, later Lady Lister, at the Tate Gallery, London. In 1624 Shoreleyker published a *Schole-house for the Needle*; the title page of the reprinted edition of 1632 says it was 'and never but once published before'. It also states that 'Here followeth certaine cut-workes, newly invented and never published before', which is rather a contradiction in terms, not unknown in publishing today. Besides geometric patterns, Shoreleyker illustrates motifs such as Adam and Eve, the Crucifixion, angels, a peacock and a pelican.

145 *Two sketches based on much more detailed designs in Johann Siebmacher's book. Two very similar figures appear in one of the Goodhart samplers*

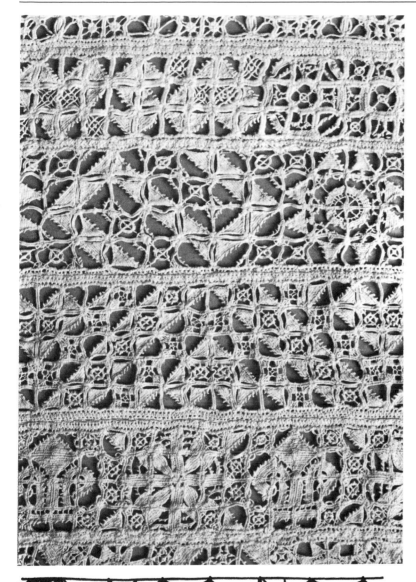

146 Part of a sampler from the mid to late seventeenth century showing considerable skill in reticella. The border in the centre is very like a pattern in the Shoreleyker book of 1632 (Embroiderers' Guild Collection)

147 Two patterns from the Shoreleyker book of 1632. Compare with the sampler

148 *An enlargement of one of five patterns on a sampler attributed to Sicily. It is in linen thread on linen fabric and each band carries a name and what appears to be a price. It is thought to be of more recent origin than the seventeenth century, possibly within the last hundred years (Embroiderers' Guild Collection)*

149 *Section of a reticella sampler showing a variety of motifs, the 'S' shape being typical and often repeated (Embroiderers' Guild Collection)*

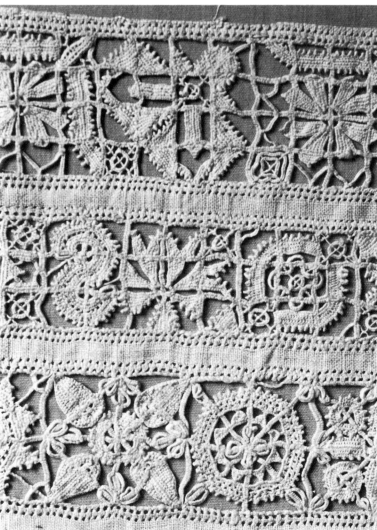

150 *(below) A motif from Shoreleyker, to compare with the sampler*

Reticella has very clear links with the beginnings of samplers, which initially formed a record of patterns as well as being a learning device. The Goodhart Collection, now housed at Montacute House in Somerset, illustrates a retrospective of sampler making from the early seventeenth century to the late nineteenth century. The collection is particularly rich in seventeenth-century samplers, several of them almost entirely devoted to reticella and 'openwork', which includes needleweaving. Number 16, worked by MC and dated 1659, is particularly beautiful and the designs are very redolent of Siebmacher. Similarly, number 29, from the same period, shows a wide range of patterns and borders. It also includes a saucy mermaid which appears on other pieces of this time. Despite the technical skill of the work it was likely to have been a learning device for 'young ladies'; in the Victoria and Albert Museum there is a very competent sampler of cut work (reticella) by Martha Edlin, aged nine in the year 1669. Prior to this she had worked a polychrome sampler, followed by a casket in 1671 and a beadwork box in 1673, when she was thirteen. Although the caskets were professionally made up, one cannot help believing that she must have been a prodigy, even although this form of training was not unusual. These samplers date from some fifty years after the standing collar was high fashion; it is likely that the collars were worked by professional broderers.

151 This is a very small fragment of a larger piece and it seems to have been an edging rather than a sampler. The work is very fine and quite different in design style from the recognised English pieces, the shapes being more flowing. Some shapes are filled solidly and some with spaced stitching (Embroiderers' Guild Collection)

152 *This sampler is particularly interesting because it is only partly worked and so the basic structure can be seen. The amusing mermaid motif appears on several samplers and is a cunning adaption of the grid (Embroiderers' Guild Collection)*

Reticella is often referred to as 'cut work' by historians. This is confusing for embroiderers, as cut work has very different connotations and methods. Reticella is clearly a drawn thread technique, but many threads are 'cut away', which explains the technical confusion.

Mutants of the technique have developed in other parts of the world as trade extended. Levkara or Lefkara lace, from a village on Cyprus, is based on the reticella technique but in a much simplified version. It is noted for rich hand-worked edgings as well as drawn thread fillings and satin stitch motifs.

Ruskin lace is also a derivative of reticella, and is sometimes known as 'Greek lace'. William Flemming and Miss Marion Twelves started the Langdale linen industry in 1883. Miss Twelves developed a form of lace based on reticella and in 1894, after moving to Keswick, she set up her own workshop for the production of this lace, to which Ruskin had happily given his name. The lace is very much alive and well today, and a high standard of competence is maintained.

In the book *Mexican Costume* by Chloe Sayer, there is an illustration showing a piece of Mexican work which is very similar to reticella in execution and design.

Working method

How is reticella constructed? Begin with a firm, closely-woven fabric. Traditionally, this was linen, but other fibres can be used, as long as they are closely woven.

The following series (figs 153–155) shows how to work an elementary square.

To work a more complex border, the method is as follows:

(1) Choose a closely woven fabric, minimum 24 threads to 2.5 cm (1 inch).

(2) Withdraw the threads. The grid size depends on the scale of the design, but as a guide, leave six or eight threads, then a space of about 3.5 cm ($1\frac{1}{2}$ inches). Make a sampler border about four spaces deep and twelve spaces long to form the basic grid.

(3) Secure the long edges with satin stitch and four-sided stitch as described earlier. Cut off any end on the wrong side.

 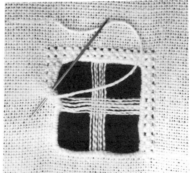

153 In this square twelve threads have been withdrawn on either side of six threads which form the central cross. Bend them under and satin stitch the edge over three threads

154 Sew a row of four-sided stitch next to the satin stitch

155 Weave half-way along the bars from the centre outwards, taking the end of the last thread from bar to bar to form a circle as shown. Buttonhole over this bar of threads, and finish the weaving. Further bars may be made in the corners by taking a thread across the corner and back again, then buttonholing over it. The foundation for the buttonholed bars is taken over the satin stitch to make it secure

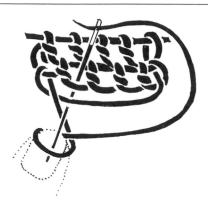

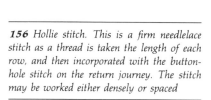

156 Hollie stitch. This is a firm needlelace stitch as a thread is taken the length of each row, and then incorporated with the button-hole stitch on the return journey. The stitch may be worked either densely or spaced

157 Another border from a sampler of five borders, probably made as a copy of an older piece, within the last hundred years. Linen on linen. The technique includes buttonhole bars, overcast bars and hollie stitch with bullion picots (Embroiderers' Guild Collection)

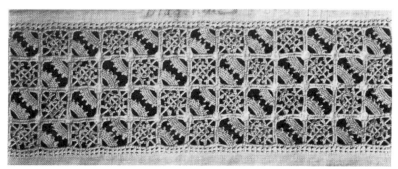

(4) Work a very open weaving in and out of the grid threads to make them firm (see the unfinished historical sampler on p. 102).

(5) This skeleton grid must now be supported in order to embroider the intricate filling. Tack the fabric to a firm, smooth background so that the needle does not catch. Historically, this was parchment, but a stiff glazed cotton or even a firm DIY plastic will be suitable. If the design is complex draw it on the background with a waterproof felt-tip pen before attaching the material. A plain blue or green background fabric is the easiest on the eye. If this backing plus material is in turn mounted on a drum or cylinder (diameter about 10 cm or 4 inches) which is padded and fabric covered, the curved surface allows the needle to scoop buttonhole stitch more easily than on a flat surface. The designs are all made by stretching a thread across the space and buttonholing back over it. For single bars, the technique has already been described on p. 103, but for filling areas hollie stitch is a good choice.

(6) When the embroidery is complete, remove the tacking stitches to free it from the background.

6 Hardanger

There are many sources of information about hardanger embroidery, with some areas of conflicting instruction. But it is generally agreed that hardanger is a highly developed peasant craft from the Hardanger region of Norway, where it is displayed on both dress and household linen.

The embroidery contrasts rich areas of satin stitch with areas of openwork in geometric forms, such as squares, triangles and diamonds. The contrast of rich surface stitchery and see-through areas forms a strong, bold texture.

Counted satin stitch is used to cover and secure the cut edges, and combines practicality and decoration. An evenweave fabric is essential for this embroidery, as the designs are counted on to it, and the technique will not work unless the counting is completely accurate. The fabric may be a simple tabby weave, or have double threads in a tabby weave (known as 'hardanger' fabric), and may nowadays be bought in colour as well as white. The best results are obtained with a single thread; pearl cotton is ideal, particularly no. 5 for the satin stitch blocks and no. 8 or *coton à broder* for the fillings. This may need to be adjusted to a choice of thinner or thicker threads depending on the fabric used. Always test on a spare piece of material first. As a rule of thumb, the thread for the satin stitch, or 'Kloster blocks', should be thicker than one thread of the ground fabric, and the thread for the fillings should match one thread of the ground fabric. Because it is sewn both vertically and horizontally, a thread with sheen or lustre enhances the play of light on the surface.

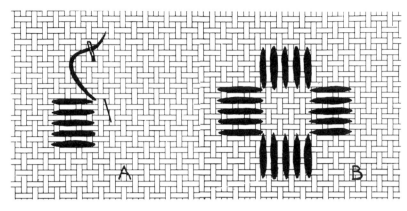

158a A Kloster block, usually five stitches over four threads

158b Four Kloster blocks, the smallest unit of design. Note how the corner stitches share a hole. When the stitching is complete, cut the threads across the middle, withdraw them to the wrong side and cut as close to the stitching as possible using a very sharp pair of scissors. Even so, little ends seem to stick out, but these disappear with the first laundering

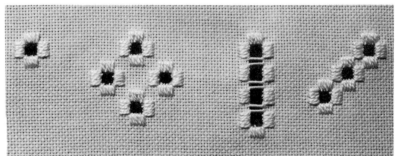

159a The smallest unit

159b Four units grouped together, each two threads away from the other

159c Shows how the Kloster blocks are worked on a larger piece, four threads being left between each Kloster block. Threads are withdrawn and cut across the width of the border only, the remaining threads being overcast

159d Simple units arranged diagonally

159e The same units in rows which could be extended to make borders or fillings

160 An edging of buttonhole stitch, with groupings of the same basic unit slotted into it. Hardanger fabric (double threads in a simple under and over weave) and pearl cotton 5

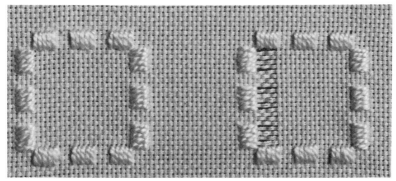

161a *Kloster blocks worked around a square leaving four threads between them. Check that Kloster blocks are aligned by following exactly on the grain from side to side, as accuracy is essential*

161b *Cut four threads and leave four threads; threads are cut only where there is a Kloster block at the end*

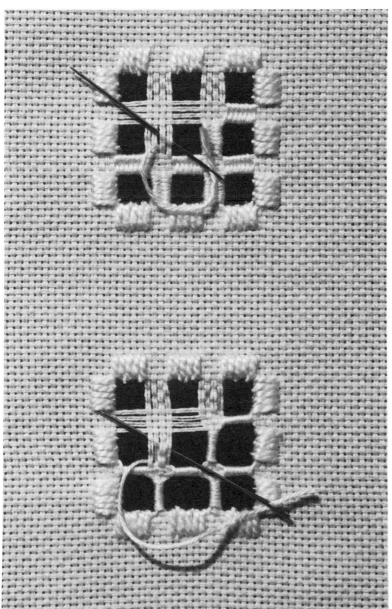

162a *The remaining threads can be woven or – **b** overcast, remembering to work diagonally. Use a thinner thread for this stitching; on this material coton à broder 18 or pearl cotton 8*

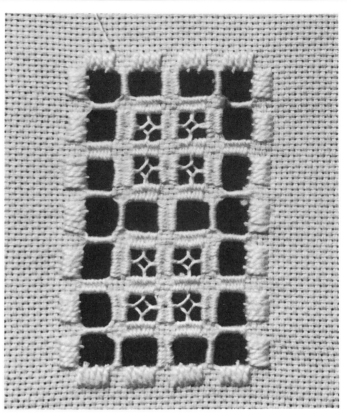

163 *A larger rectangle incorporating over-casting, weaving and crosses made of four blanket stitches (Greek cross)*

164 *A larger motif; in this case the satin stitch is worked in four stitches over four threads, five stitches over eight threads and then four stitches over four again, to form one side. Four threads are withdrawn, four left, and four withdrawn, in each direction to form the centre. Buttonhole is then worked as shown with a small eyelet in the centre*

165 *Completed motif*

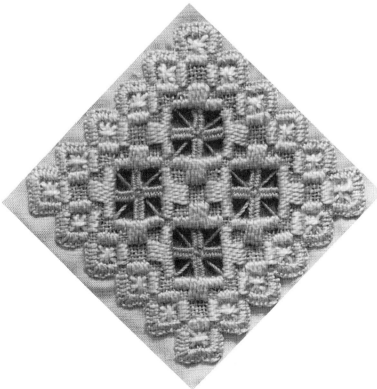

166 *Design incorporating four motifs similar to the one above with double cross stitches and a buttonhole edge, which would make an attractive pincushion. The design could be repeated, without the buttonhole edge, to form the border on a cushion or table mat (By Heide Jenkins; Embroiderers' Guild Collection)*

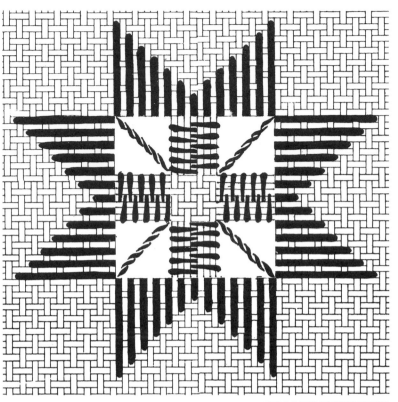

167 A star-shaped motif made by decreasing and increasing the length of the satin stitch by one thread as shown in the diagram. Four threads are withdrawn, four left and four withdrawn in both directions to form the centre; the four threads left are woven, and overcast bars added in the corners

168 The completed motif

189 *Formal motifs could be worked randomly as decoration on a bag or cushion*

170 *Picots are small knobs added to the edges of stitchery to elaborate the texture; bullion and buttonhole picots have already been described but a looped picot is the simplest. (A) Weave some way along a bar and make a stitch as shown. (B) Pull the thread upward, but leave slackness to make the picot loop and continue weaving*

171 *(left) A diamond-shaped motif with Kloster blocks in 'steps' to make the outline. Within this shape four threads are withdrawn, and four left, as in previous fillings, and then decorated with stitchery*

172 *(right) This is an elongated diamond with quarter eyelets and picots added. This motif could be repeated in a zigzag fashion to become a border or filling*

173 Hardanger fillings richly worked with picots and additional woven bars. The stages of building up the filling can be seen in the partly worked sections (By Heide Jenkins; Embroiderers' Guild Collection)

174 By using triangles and squares of hardanger, stylised houses may be designed. Although the overall shape of each house remains the same, the fillings may be varied

175 A formally arranged pattern makes an attractive practical mat. Always begin borders in the centre of one side and work outwards to the edge to ensure symmetry. The edge on this mat is made of woven bars, folded in half on to the wrong side to make outsize picots (Embroiderers' Guild Collection)

1 *A miniature portrait of Frances Sidney by Henry Bone, in enamel on copper. Notice the reticella collar and cuffs (The National Trust Photographic Library)*

2 *A sampler of borders. Coloured silk floss threads have been used largely to form the borders on linen in a variety of different stitches. Some of the motifs are very similar to those of seventeenth-century monochrome reticella (Victoria and Albert Museum)*

3 *A withdrawn grid on white fabric with vari-coloured buttonhole stitch covering the bars. Beads are suspended on transparent thread worked diagonally on the basic grid. The whole piece is backed with a random check fabric (Emroiderers' Guild Collection)*

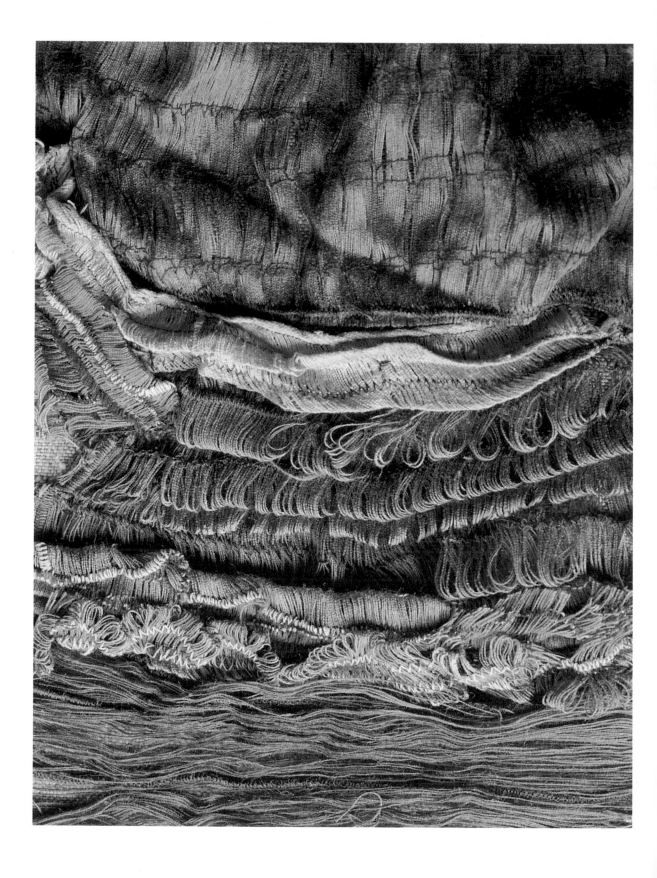

5 *A small, sensitively worked embroidery based on a withdrawn cross. Needleweaving has been worked into the remaining fabric in a variety of thread thicknesses and subtle colours, and then embellished with beads and tassels (Carolyn Batts, Embroiderers' Guild Collection)*

4 *(opposite) A combination of rich textural surfaces forms a panel suggesting landscape. The weft of dupion is chemically dissolved after tucks and ridges have been machine sewn (Maureen Wade)*

6 (opposite) A bag with a very richly encrusted surface. The layers include metallic fabric bonded on to calico, held down with a web of silver zigzag, black and white paint stencilled through canvas, free black zigzag whip stitch, looping with the tailor tacking foot, threads withdrawn from grey evenweave fabric in a regular grid, the remaining machine thread wrapped, and then the ribbon threaded through and knotted. The fringe of ribbons on the lower edge is knotted on. All these techniques combine to create a sumptious surface (Valerie Campbell-Harding)

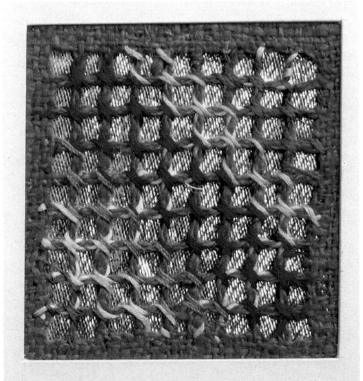

7 A grid is withdrawn on a bold blue fabric and then worked in a diagonal filling in rainbow colouring. Gold lurex backs the embroidery, making it rich and exotic (June Linsley)

8 *Dupions with chemically withdrawn threads, which were then manipulated, are the basis of this rich textural surface (Maureen Wade)*

176 Leaf shapes have been painted on pink hardanger in a range of greens. Hardanger motifs are then spattered over this, like flowers in an herbaceous border in soft pinks and mauves (Helen Wadsley)

177 A richly encrusted border worked diag onally across the fabric in steps. The centre need not be cut out, when it could be the decorative edge of a tie or scarf

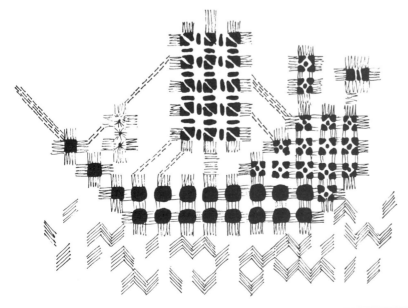

178 With a bit of imagination, amusing motifs can be worked, even within the strict confines of the technique. It is best to plan these on graph paper first to check on the overall shape and proportions

7 Experimental drawn thread

It is generally assumed that in drawn thread techniques a fabric is used from which threads can be removed, so that the remaining 'bars' of thread can be manipulated into groups, twisted or woven. The purpose of removing threads is to create bars on which to work. Can these bars be created in any other way? If a non-fray fabric, such as pelmet interfacing, felt or leather, is used and slits cut in it to form bars, these can be twisted, tied or woven in a manner similar to formal drawn thread techniques. As the edges do not need to be secured, the shape is not limited to the vertical and horizontal threads of a woven fabric, but can also be curved.

It may be necessary to bond an interlining, such as *staflex*, to interfacing and felt to give them flexibility and strength. Alternatively, a fabric like calico can be bonded to the felt with *bondaweb*. It is advisable to add a backing if the bars are narrow or if they are to be twisted, as bought felt is often weak and can split under pressure. If a contrasting coloured fabric is bonded on, a flash of the colour will show when the twists are made. The system of tying and twisting is exactly the same as that described for working borders on pp. 27–30.

Needleweaving on the cut bars with either yarn or fabric strips is a further possibility. As the weaving adds additional bulk, it will be necessary to trim down the width of the bars if a flat surface is required in the finished piece. Otherwise, why not accept the unevenly raised surface which emerges from the technique?

Plastics, whether clear or coloured, could also be used for this form of drawn thread experiment.

'Free' ends
Another assumption is that once threads have been withdrawn to the edge of a shape they must be cut off, darned in or organised in some way.

As the threads are withdrawn the tension created by pulling and stretching makes them curl attractively. In a purely decorative piece they could be left in this state. If the threads need to be more permanently positioned, they can be couched in position. If a very

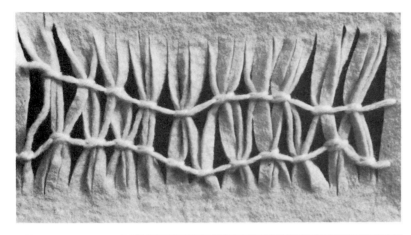

179a Slits are cut in felt and these are tied randomly with a woollen yarn. The stitch is the same as for a tied border

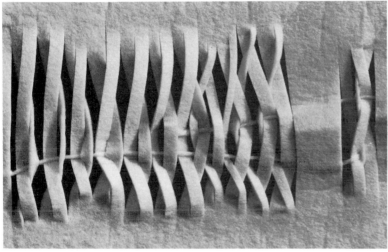

179b Slits cut in pelmet interfacing, a thick interlining; the resulting 'bars' have been twisted

179c Slits also cut in pelmet interfacing and in this case tied on the wrong side. If felt or interfacing is dampened, coloured paints or inks can be added and allowed to merge into each other giving a space-dyed effect. Dry flat on a sheet of plastic; the colour will bleed out of these fabrics or drip off them if they are hung up

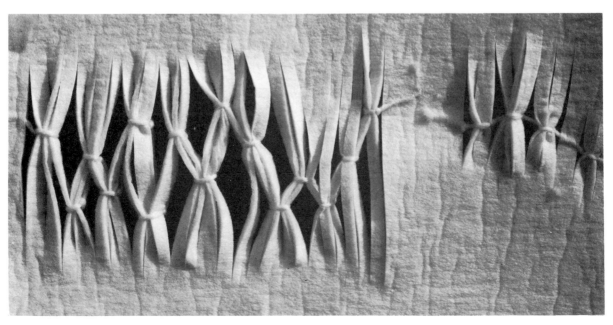

180 *If you look at car headlamps, the lens is made up of a series of lines or blocks. This is a drawing from a car headlamp giving an interesting selection of angles and spacing; the dotted lines indicate the area chosen as a basis for design*

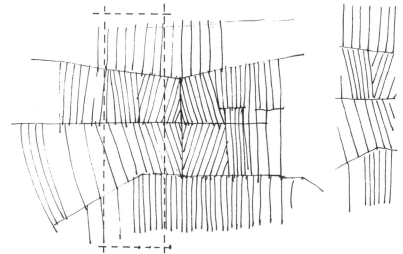

181 *Tracing lines within the dotted area*

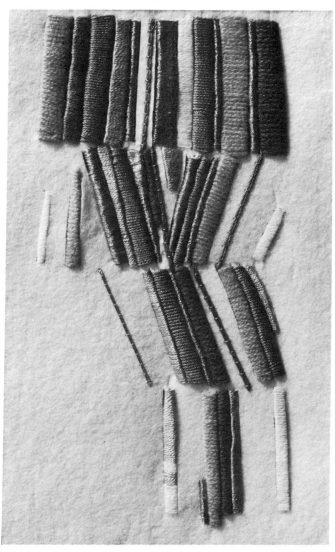

182 *Not all the lines were selected, but slits were made in pelmet interfacing for those that were. The resulting 'bars' were then overcast with coloured knitting yarns and metal threads, and some thinner couched lines added*

fine or invisible thread is used for the couching, the free and lively appearance can be retained.

183 Threads withdrawn from a mixed polyester and linen fabric, curling as they are withdrawn from the fabric

184 A sketched idea to suggest one way in which the curled threads can form part of a design as the hair surrounding a face

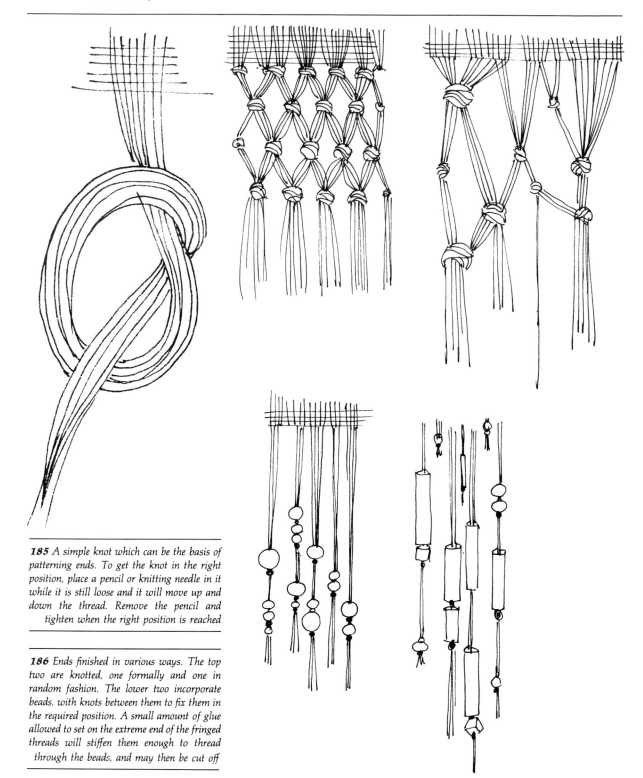

185 A simple knot which can be the basis of patterning ends. To get the knot in the right position, place a pencil or knitting needle in it while it is still loose and it will move up and down the thread. Remove the pencil and tighten when the right position is reached

186 Ends finished in various ways. The top two are knotted, one formally and one in random fashion. The lower two incorporate beads, with knots between them to fix them in the required position. A small amount of glue allowed to set on the extreme end of the fringed threads will stiffen them enough to thread through the beads, and may then be cut off

If the threads are long enough, they can form a surface decoration by being:

- formed into a tassel; a block of straight stitch worked across the threads creates a tassel effect
- knotted to form a fringe
- macraméd (if really long)
- pulled under a block of threads – evenly or randomly – using a fine crochet hook
- freely woven back into some of the fabric to create a rough, irregular texture
- interspersed with other threads either to add contrast in weight or colour, or to make a thick fringe of threads which may then be tasselled, knotted, etc. as described earlier
- threaded with beads and held in place with a simple knot

187 Ends formed into a tassel

188 Ends pulled evenly through a block of threads

189 Another face framed by hair, formed by withdrawn ends; in this example the threads have been pulled straight and could be held down with couching or zigzag machining

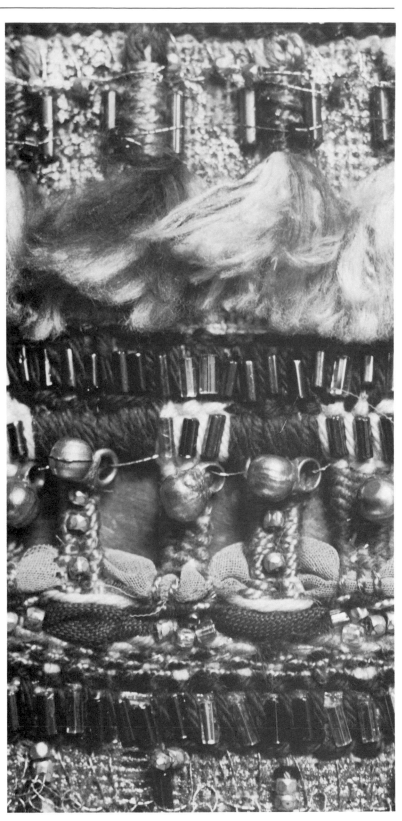

190 A richly encrusted surface, which includes needlewoven bars, needleweaving with fabric strips and threads, applied beads of differing shapes and surface buttonhole stitch in very fine metal thread. Colours such as beige, terracotta, dull red and blue combine to make this a delightfully conceived and executed miniature embroidery (Embroiderers' Guild Collection)

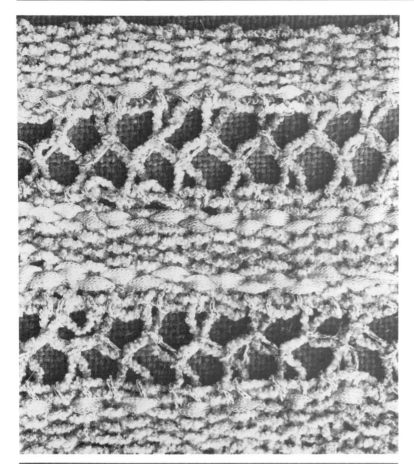

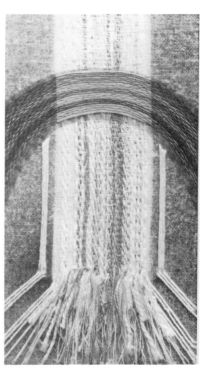

191 Tied zigzag border and threads woven into knitting make this an inventive combination of techniques in pleasant bluey colouring (June Linsley)

192 (above) A stylised waterfall and rainbow. The threads were withdrawn from a wide band and the ends allowed to hang. A great variety of threads was woven into the withdrawn band and allowed to hang free. The rainbow is running stitch on transparent fabric

193 A stand of trees in natural hessian; threads have been withdrawn and the remainder overcast to form trunks. Threads from the fabric have been looped to make the leaves and foliage (Jean Drostle)

194 A design based on repeated shapes of a leaping figure. Sprayed paper and scrim (Jean Drostle)

195 A panel based on the design. Figures are laid on the background and invisibly held in position. An inch in front of this is a piece of scrim that has had threads withdrawn almost entirely in one direction to form a misty layer; ends have been left free to float to emphasise the feeling of movement (Jean Drostle)

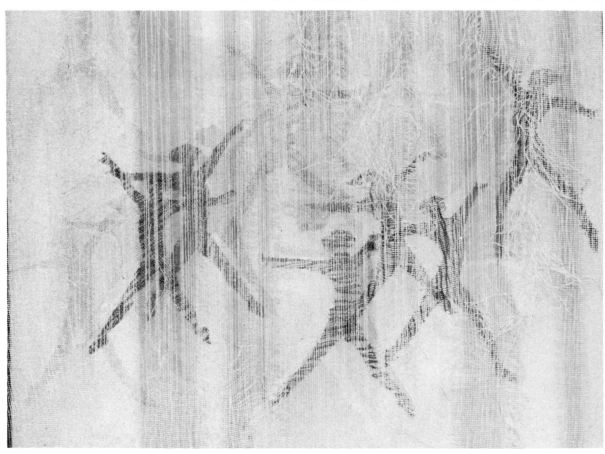

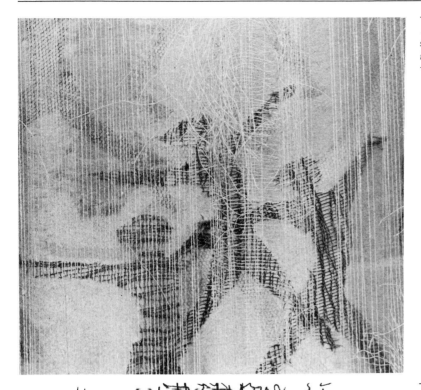

197 *A sketchbook drawing of a dense wood*

198 *A possible interpretation of the sketch would be to withdraw threads horizontally, and buttonhole the trunks of the trees; another option would be to consider the withdrawn bands as the tree trunks and the buttonhole stitch as foliage*

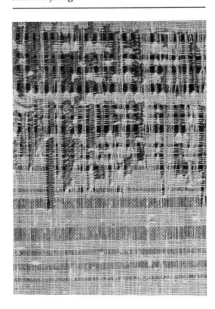

Chemically dissolving threads

This technique was invented by Maureen Wade during her City and Guilds course; she saw the potential of dissolving threads instead of laboriously withdrawing them. For this method it is essential that the fabric has an acetate yarn in one direction and a non-acetate yarn (e.g. polyester or cotton) in the opposite direction. The fabric Maureen based her experiments on was a dupion, which has an acetate warp that dissolves in acetone.

In order to assess whether a fabric is suitable, immerse a sample of it in a jar, preferably one with a tight screw-top lid, filled with acetone. Acetone is a chemical that should be used with great care in a very well ventilated area; it is also extremely flammable, so keep it away from any naked flame.

As half the fabric will be dissolved, it is obvious that the remaining threads will have to be secured in some way to prevent total disintegration.

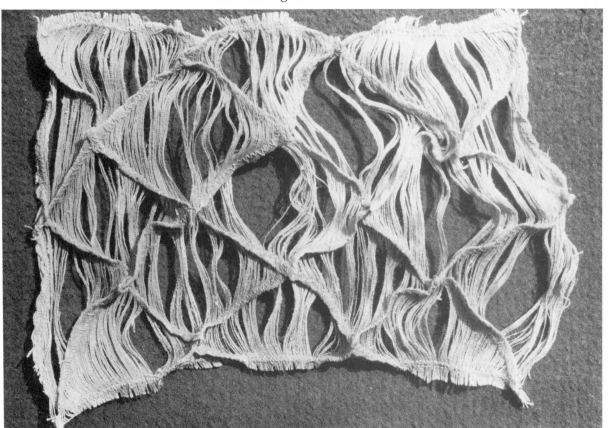

199 *Fabric tucked in diamonds and the weft dissolved*

Some of the methods Maureen used in her experiments were:

(1) Fold the material to form tucks, and machine these in place with either straight stitch or zigzag. The tucks can be in straight parallel rows, in diagonal lines, a diagonal grid, or a vertical/horizontal grid.

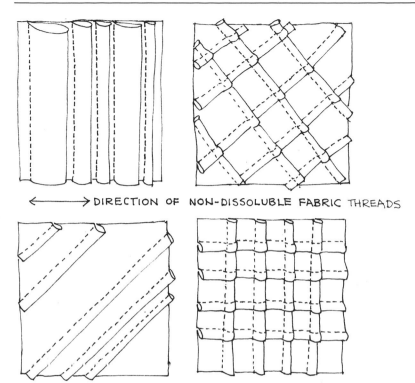

← ──→ DIRECTION OF NON-DISSOLUBLE FABRIC THREADS

200 Ways of machine tucking fabric

After dunking the tucked fabric in an acetone bath until the required threads have dissolved, take it out and blot off any excess with a paper towel. While the result is drying, pull and manipulate it to shape. Leave it to dry fully on a paper towel or newspaper, but do not press it down, or it will bond with the paper.

(2) Another experiment is to 'patch' fabrics of contrasting colours together in a crazy patchwork fashion. Overlap one piece with its neighbour without turning in an edge, and zigzag over this seam with a wide, close stitch. Lastly, zigzag around the edge of the whole piece. Dissolve as already described and manipulate the piece into shape as it dries.

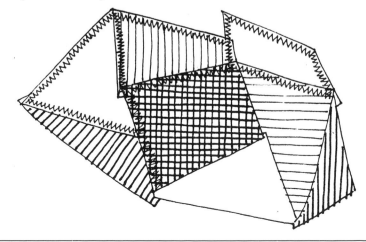

201 Different coloured fabrics patched and partly machine zigzagged (idea by Maureen Wade)

(3) A leaf or feather form may be achieved by joining two elliptical shapes together so that their grains go in opposing directions. Zigzag down the centre with a close, wide zigzag and around the outer edge. Dissolve as previously described and manipulate the piece into shape as it dries.

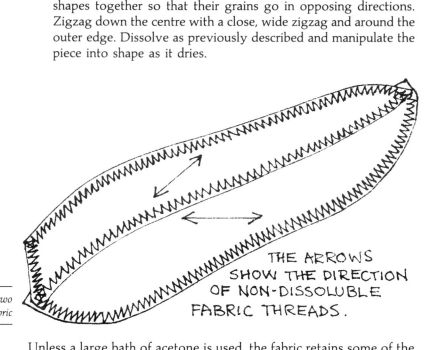

THE ARROWS SHOW THE DIRECTION OF NON-DISSOLUBLE FABRIC THREADS.

202 A leaf shape, or feather joining two pieces of fabric

203 Showing the sort of textures and shapes derived from Maureen Wade's experiments

Unless a large bath of acetone is used, the fabric retains some of the melted acetate and will therefore be stiff when it dries. This technique is therefore particularly suitable for three-dimensional work, which needs to be self-supporting.

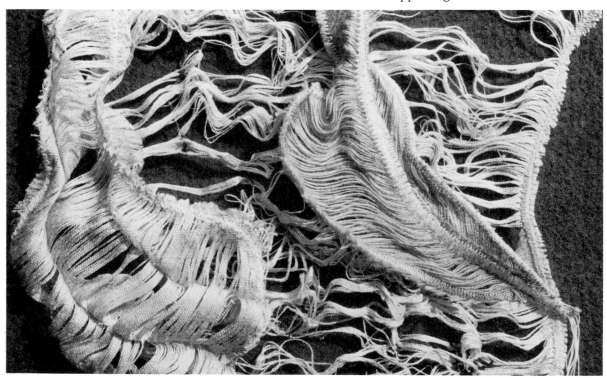

This method can be just the beginning of a piece of work. Its surface can be enriched with stitches, such as raised chain band and raised stem stitch band, where the stiff threads of the ground could be used as the 'ladder' which supports these stitches. Sections of stiffened fabric can be applied together with softer fabrics or on canvas in conjunction with canvas stitches.

Acetone can be obtained from a chemist; always remember that it is a very volatile chemical so it must be used in a very well ventilated area, very far away from any form of flame or spark.

Colour in drawn thread

In the past drawn thread has been linked with monochromatic work, that is, all one colour, often white or off-white.

Shot fabric, that is material woven with one colour in the warp and another in the weft, will emphasise one colour when warp threads are withdrawn, and another when weft threads are removed. For example, red and blue warp and weft threads combine to form a purple or mauve fabric, but the red and blue will reappear as separate colours in withdrawn bands or borders.

Striped fabrics can also be stimulating. The stripe will probably be intensified in colour in a band that is withdrawn at right angles to it. Or the stripe width and pattern can be altered if one colour of stripe is removed. For these effects it is, of course, essential that the stripe is woven into the fabric and not just printed on it.

In the past it has been customary for drawn thread to be worked on a plain fabric, but why not use patterned? Patchwork can combine a variety of patterns successfully; so why not other forms of textile decoration?

Nowadays, products are available that give considerable opportunity for colouring fabric and threads at home. Many of these can be made permanent simply by ironing with a hot iron after being applied with a brush. Trying to match thread to fabric can lead to a prolonged search, not always ending in success. If white threads and fabrics are immersed in the same dye bath, the resulting colours, if not matching, will at least be sympathetic.

Even more interesting varied fabric and thread can be produced by space-dyeing both at the same time. Space-dyeing involves two or three colours merging into each other in the dye bath, so that fabric and thread are subtlely multicoloured. By working on this fabric with similar thread, the rigidity of drawn thread borders and fillings is overcome so that they look much softer.

Another option is to colour the fabric after the embroidery has been worked. To improve the penetration of the dye it is a good idea to damp the embroidery well beforehand; this helps the colour to bleed into the stitchery as well as the fabric. The colour can be plain or space-dyed.

If localised colour only is desired, then dye or paint can be sponged or painted on. A fairly dry sponge dipped into a fabric paint will give a texture as well as colour. Felt-tip pens can also be used for localised colour, but they may not be permanent. If the fabric is damped well, the felt-tip colour will spread, especially if a broad tip is used, whereas colouring directly on fabric with a felt-tip will show each stroke, making an interesting texture.

Spraying is another method of colouring. For basic, direct spraying, car paint aerosols are excellent. They do not make the fabric hard unless used to excess — usually a quick squirt is all that is needed to make quite intense colour. Spray from about 30 cm (12 inches) away to diffuse the spray; it is not 'permanent', but will wash several times. For really controlled spraying, an air-brush is advisable as the nozzle can be controlled to spray in either a diffused or a concentrated way. Spraying raised surfaces, such as the Maureen Wade experiments, can enhance the three-dimensional effect by creating a permanent shadow. Spray from low down on one side for the most dramatic effect.

8 Machine drawn thread

Machine stitching has already been mentioned as useful for securing edges, being quicker and often firmer than hand stitching. Machine embroidery is not just an adjunct to hand embroidery, however; it is also a craft in its own right, using techniques that are not necessarily based on hand methods. In this chapter, both aspects of machine embroidery are described.

A 'hemstitch' needle is available for machine mock hem stitch; the needle is very thick above the point so that it punches a hole in the fabric as well as stitching. It works best on a fine, crisp, closely woven fabric such as organdie; on softer, more resilient materials the hole tends to close up after it has been punched.

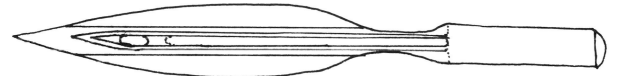

204 Shape of hemstitch machine needle

The procedure is: turn up a single hem about 0.5 cm ($\frac{1}{4}$ inch) wider than the finished hem. Pin or tack in position. Work a row of stitching using the hemstitch needle; this may be a simple straight stitch but is more effective as a zigzag. Additional variation can be achieved by use of a set pattern machine stitch. Tie off the ends. Trim off any excess fabric close to the stitching with a sharp pair of scissors.

Before trimming, more than one row of stitching may be machined to make a more decorative hem, but it is not easy to make successive rows match exactly and echo the first row of stitching, because the first row tends to pucker slightly and tension the fabric.

There is also a twin hemstitch needle where one needle is ordinary and the other hemstitch. It is used in much the same way as the single hemstitch needle, but it must be remembered that a full width zigzag or pattern cannot be used, as the needle will hit the plate and break.

To make this kind of machine stitch more effective, a narrow band

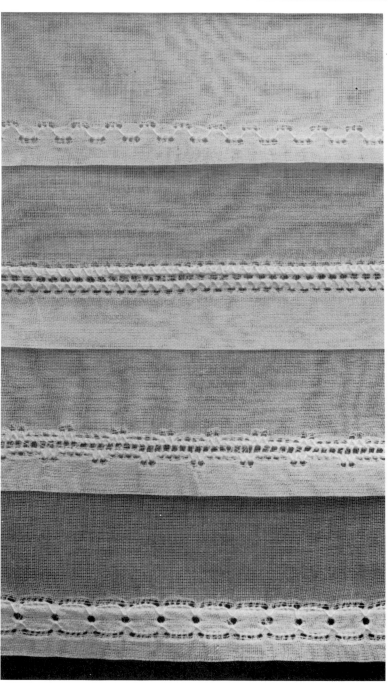

205a *Simple pattern with hemstitch needle*

205b *Two rows of zigzag with hemstitch needle*

205c *Two rows of pattern back to back, with hemstitch needle*

205d *Two rows of pattern facing each other, with hemstitch needle*
(All the examples are worked on organdie)

of threads may be withdrawn and the mock hemstitch worked down one side of the band. This technique could also be used to secure a turned hem.

Machining with the foot on – fillings

Many drawn thread fillings are based on a grid: for example, alternately withdrawing four threads, leaving four threads. The remaining threads are then whipped or wrapped, which can be very laborious and time-consuming if done by hand, but is much quicker and equally effective by machine. Zigzag stitch replaces hand whipping or wrapping. Choose a fairly closely woven fabric.

(1) Work two rows of straight stitching very close together around the outline
(2) Withdraw the threads up to this machining and cut them off neatly
(3) Set the machine to zigzag (the width will depend on the threads to be covered). Work up and down the filling in an orderly fashion until all is complete

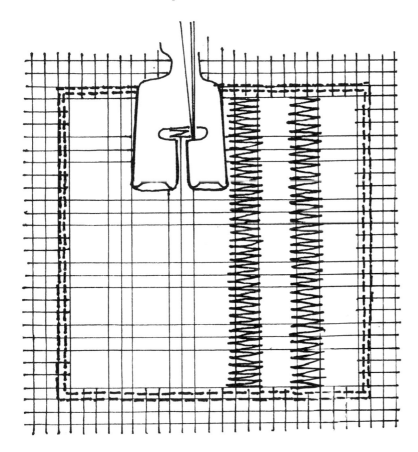

206 Stages 1 to 3 with the foot zigzagging the bars

(4) Zigzag over the straight stitching around the edge

By backing the material with a firm substance, the machining can be made easier to manage. Suitable materials for this are tissue paper, vanishing muslin (a chemically treated muslin that disintegrates when a hot iron is applied) or stitch 'n' tear (this resembles a stiff interlining and, as its name suggests, is torn away when the work is complete).

The fillings may be further elaborated with intersecting lines of straight stitching across the spaces.

Free machining

For much machine embroidery, the 'free' mode is employed. This is often described under 'darning' in the machine manual; refer to the instructions.

In general terms, the procedure is:

(1) Remove the foot
(2) Lower or cover the feed-dog (teeth); if the feed-dog cannot be lowered, a cover plate is either provided or can be bought for most machines
(3) Set the stitch length to zero
(4) *Always* put the take-up lever *down* (which normally operates the foot) before stitching, otherwise the tension will be affected
(5) Place the material in a circular frame (bind the inner ring with tape, this will hold the fabric firmer). Make sure the fabric sits flat on the bed of the machine by lowering the inner frame just below the level of the outer one

There should be no need to alter the tension from normal; to begin use ordinary sewing thread in both top and spool. Always test the stitch on an oddment of fabric before starting on the real thing. After confidence has been gained with ordinary sewing threads, there are many different kinds of special machine embroidery threads that can be used. For these, it may be necessary to adjust the tension, but do this only by minimal movements, as described in the machine manual. Test the stitch after each adjustment.

To begin: place the frame under the needle and take one stitch to bring up the spool thread to the surface. Make several stitches on the spot to anchor the thread. Cut off the ends close to the fabric. The frame may now be moved in any direction. Hold it lightly so that it moves easily.

Needleweaving

Withdraw a band of threads about 2.5 cm (1 inch) wide. Put the fabric in a frame. Start as previously described. Set the zigzag width to about 3 mm ($\frac{1}{8}$ inch).

Work up and down the bars of withdrawn threads; the zigzag will group them. Try moving diagonally. To make a thicker 'band', go over the stitching two or three times. This random technique tends to look like trees, twigs or bare hedgerows.

An extension of this idea is to machine around a predetermined shape with two rows of straight stitch, very close together. Within this shape, withdraw the threads in one direction and work over the remaining threads as before. The result suggests a cellular structure or trees, twigs, etc. The edge can be made more secure by working a zigzag over it. If, say, three pieces were worked in this way in different colours, they could be layered to give a three-dimensional effect.

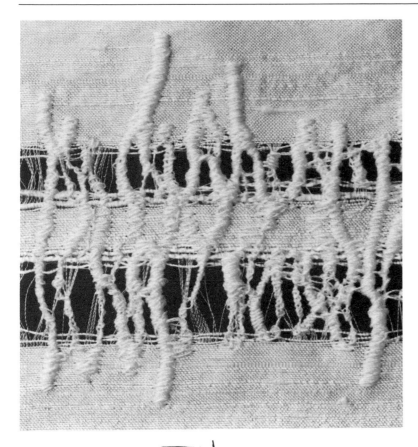

207 *Two bands of threads withdrawn from pure silk fabric and zigzag worked over the remaining threads, with the width set*

208 *Material in a frame with free zigzag machining taking place. The irregular shape is stay-stitched with straight machine stitching before threads are withdrawn. The fabric is mounted in a circular frame with the inner ring bound*

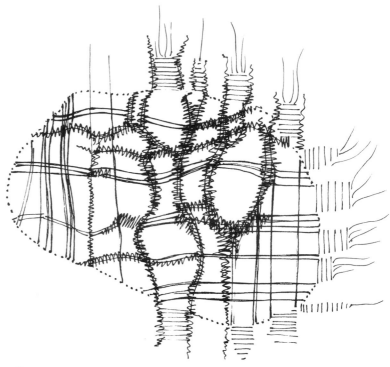

209 Threads withdrawn randomly in both directions; the remaining threads are then zigzagged to group them

Fillings

Prepare an area by withdrawing threads in both directions as described on p. 53. Patterns can then be formed on the remaining threads in a variety of ways.

210 A machine filling echoing the hand method. Bars are zigzagged and stars and crosses worked between them in free machining (June Linsley)

It is quite possible to machine across a space as long as there is an anchoring point at either side; but with the advent of cold- and hot-water-soluble fabrics this is made easier by a foundation that will later disappear.

Cold-water-soluble fabric (*Solvi*) resembles a thin transparent plastic. It must be stretched very tightly or it will rip and tear, and generally misbehave. Its great advantage is that it dissolves very easily in cold water.

Hot-water-soluble fabric resembles a pale blue organza and is much easier to machine on but, because it needs very hot water to dissolve it, can shrink some materials and threads. To dissolve thoroughly, it may need to be simmered gently.

Bearing these points in mind, either of these types of fabric can be used to support stitching where much of the fabric has been removed. Simply put the soluble fabric underneath the main fabric in the frame, and stitch through both. Remember that the backing fabric will disappear and therefore all the stitched lines must connect or holes will appear where not required! Holding the work up to the light and scanning it closely usually reveals any discrepancies.

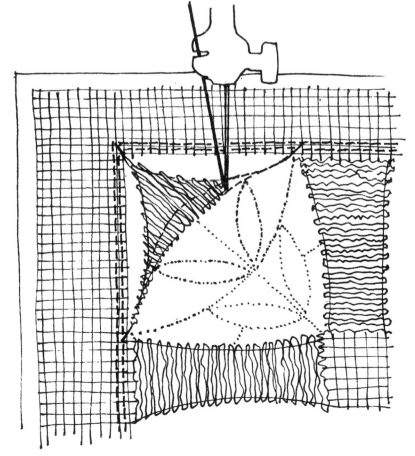

211 *Close-up of an area of machine reticella in the working. The dotted line is the pattern drawn on to the soluble backing with a water-soluble felt-tip fabric marker*

Machine reticella is an extension of the previous technique. Use a fairly closely woven fabric. Mark out a square or rectangle with chalk or a water-soluble fabric felt-tip pen. Decide which areas are to be removed and which left; this may be done by measuring rather than counting – for example, 1.75 cm ($\frac{5}{8}$ inch) removed, 1 cm ($\frac{3}{8}$ inch) left. Secure the edge with two or three rows of straight stitch, close together. Withdraw threads; the remaining bars can be grouped by being zigzagged over or straight stitched across.

Now back the fabric with soluble fabric, if it is to be used. Using a water-soluble pen, trace the rest of the pattern to be worked, if it is intricate, on the backing fabric. To construct a solid or filled shape, work two or three lines of straight stitch at right angles to the direction of the final stitching and then work over them in straight stitch. Never work zigzag without straight stitch underlying it, otherwise when the dissoluble fabric disappears the zigzag pulls into a straight line!

Lastly, neaten the edge by covering the initial straight stitching with zigzag. Make sure all the stitched lines are connected before dissolving the backing. Gently pull the piece into shape and allow to dry on a flat surface.

If it is necessary to press the work, put it face down on several layers of blanket or a similar soft surface and iron with a steam iron or damp cloth, easing the embroidery back into shape.

212 Detail of machine reticella

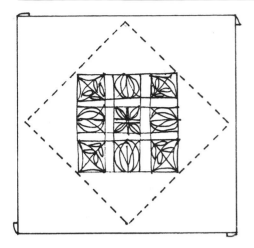

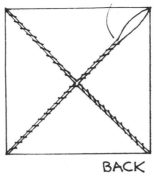

BACK

213 Planning the machine reticella pin-cushion. The embroidery is centred on a piece of fabric. The dotted line shows the actual pincushion size. Edges are turned under once. The back view shows how the corners meet and the seams are oversewn

214 The pincushion finished, with ribbon-like knitting yarn threaded and knotted to make a textural contrast. Imitation linen dress fabric in beige, paler beige embroidery and ribbon in pastel colouring

Following on from this process, which is based closely on traditional reticella, a much more free approach can be adopted.

- The grid of withdrawn threads need not be even: it is possible to leave very few threads, in fact, the bare minimum for support, allowing for a less formal design concept in the remaining spaces.
- Rather than working in monochrome, colour could be introduced.

Although machine techniques can develop from hand embroidery, essentially the medium is quite different. All embroidery has to start from a basis of shapes, that is, design, and the technique

215 Aviary; a panel worked in the machine reticella method on a widely spaced grid. The simplified bird shapes change colour as the bars cross them, and the twigs are added to complete the design and also to hold the work together. On a pale green evenweave linen, with multicoloured birds

evolves from the texture and colour needed to decorate those shapes. It was this design basis that suggested textural development. Reflections in surfaces of all sorts, whether rounded shapes like jugs and kettles, flat shapes like glass-clad tower blocks or the rippled surfaces of water, all offer endless permutations and options.

216 Sketch of reflected shapes in a leaded window, that is, one with small panes

Grid structures are linked to drawn thread because of the vertical and horizontal withdrawal of warp and weft threads, but is it necessary to dispose of all the ends neatly? While withdrawing threads for a design based on a grid structure of reflections of a figure in tiles, it became apparent that leaving them uncut meant that the rigid grid was softened, and the following process developed:

(1) The grid structure was marked on the fabric, making sure it was square on the grain. The grid was then zigzagged with a fairly open stitch, keeping on the grain as far as possible.

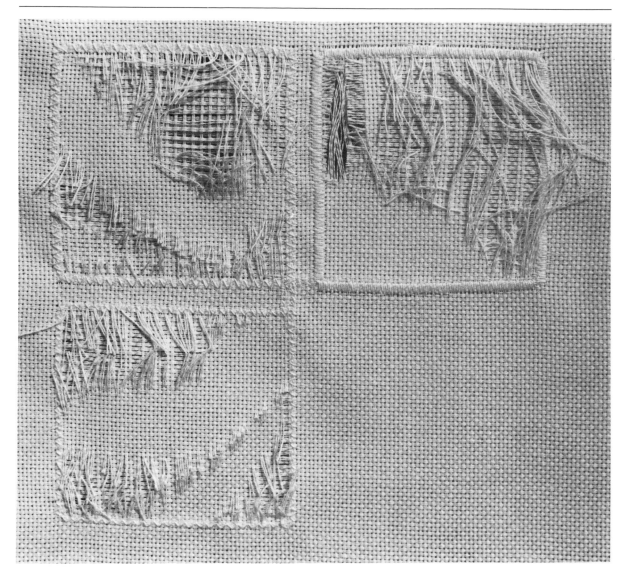

217 *Threads look free and attractive when withdrawn and left to lie where they will. The three squares shown here are experiments towards interpreting the shapes of the reflections, with differing weights of zigzag securing the edge*

(2) Some of the areas within each block of the grid were to be left as solid fabric, so threads were cut in the centre of each block in a random fashion. These were then withdrawn to the edge.
(3) The withdrawn threads were then bent back out of the way and held back with sticky tape, straight stitch machining was then worked to group the remaining threads.
(4) All the negative (background) shapes were machined in this way, and the sellotaped threads released.
(5) The remaining positive shapes were hand embroidered in simple stitchery, mainly running stitch.

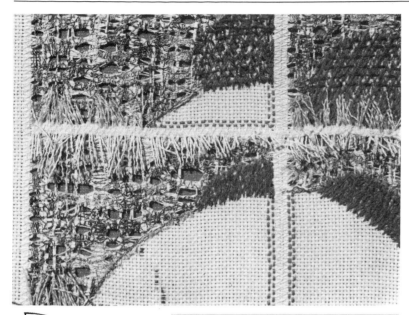

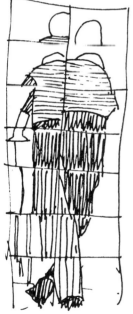

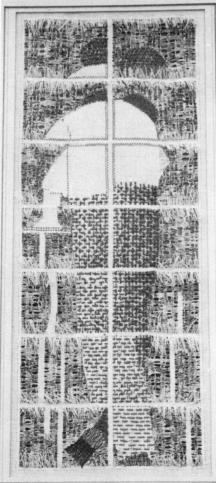

218 *A detail showing the technique described in 1 to 5*

219 *Quick sketch of a figure reflected in tiles*

220 *The finished panel combining hand and machine techniques*

221 A small bag made from plastic sacking in beige; threads have been withdrawn and machine zigzagged in gold as well as rows of stitching worked directly on to the fabric. Tassels in Twilleys Goldfingering are attached along the flap (Mrs J. Edwards)

Further reading

One Man's Samplers, The Goodhart Collection, London Borough of Richmond upon Thames Libraries Department
Manuale del Cucito e del Ricamo, Coats, Milan
La Broderie Nationale Bulgare, Imprimerie D'Etat
Drawn Thread Work, Thèrese de Dillmont, DMC Library
Drawn Thread Work (second series), Thèrese de Dillmont, DMC Library
Hardanger Embroideries, DMC Library
Broderies Ajourées sur Toile, DMC Library
Historical Designs for Embroidery, Louisa F. Pesel, B. T. Batsford Ltd
Weldon's Encyclopaedia of Needlework, Waverley
Encyclopaedia of Needlework, Thèrese de Dillmont, DMC Library
The Embroideress, Volume Five
The Needlewoman Embroidery Book No. I
The Needleworker's Dictionary, Pamela Clabburn, Macmillan London Ltd
The Identification of Lace, Pat Earnshaw, Shire Publications Ltd
A Schole-house for the Needle, Richard Shorleyker, 1632
Newes Modelbuch, Johann Siebmacher, 1604
Lace, Santina Levey
Handbook of English Costume in the Sixteenth Century, C. W. & P. Cunningham
The Royal School of Needlework Book of Needlework and Embroidery, Collins
Lace, Virginia Churchill, Bath, Studio Vista

Index